Nicholas Moussis

The European Union with or without a Constitution:

A response to citizens' questions

European Study Service

ISBN
2-930119-39-X

Avenue Paola 43 - B-1330 RIXENSART
TEL.: (+32 2) 652 02 84 - FAX: (+32 2) 653 01 80
RCN: 51147 - TVA: BE-659 309 394

SUMMARY

CONTENTS

INTRODUCTION

A picture can tell a story better than a thousand words. One such picture illustrates the lack of interest of people for a historic event that takes place under their very eyes. It is a painting of 1564 A.D. by the Flemish master Pieter Bruegel the elder. It is called "Christ bearing the cross". If it was not for its title one would hardly notice Christ in the picture. He is, in fact, a small figure sinking down under the cross on his way up the hill towards the place of crucifixion. Although He is in the very centre of the picture, no one of the hundreds of Roman soldiers and ordinary people around Him pays any attention to Him. They are all looking at a couple of peasants struggling with three soldiers in the forefront of the picture. This ordinary brawl is the centre of interest of the crowd and not the event that has marked the history of mankind. One can hardly blame these people who, at the time of the Crucifixion, were going about their business and were attracted by a boisterous albeit banal happening. As shown by Brueguel, they had not the hindsight that we now have about the importance of the event that they were witnessing.

Can we then blame contemporary Europeans for their lack of interest in European integration? Have they any notion that they are participating in **an event that will most probably change again the course of history**. This history is marked by wars and conflicts of all kinds, of bloody fights between ethnic, religious and other groups, fights for power, for land, for ideals (real or supposed) or just for the survival of a nation or a group attacked by other nations or groups. The exceptional event that occurs in front of our eyes is the fifty-year old experience of peaceful and voluntary unification of different and at one time conflicting nations. Yet this event is hardly exciting. It is hidden behind tedious negotiations by complicated institutions ending in legal texts written in a language incomprehensible to ordinary citizens. Contemporary Europeans are not to blame - any more than the spectators in Brueguel's painting - for going about their business, for being worried about the myriad problems of their everyday lives and for showing more interest in the petty events taking place in their vicinity rather than in the big event that may be a milestone for mankind.

Yet, contemporary Europeans could have a better perception of the importance of European unification, if they had better information about its scope and achievements to date, notably lasting peace among their previously antagonistic nations, respect for human rights and the rule of law, the economic development and social protection promoted by the European Community/Union. The problem is that **citizens take for granted the benefits that they enjoy** and the many rights that they have acquired thanks to European integration, particularly the right to a peaceful, liberal and legally secured existence. For most Europeans, the peaceful coexistence and emulation of different European nations is self-evident and not to be attributed to unfamiliar Treaties, policies or common legislation [see section 7.1.3].

Uninterested citizens tend to forget the tariffs and other barriers hindering trade and therefore limiting their choice of goods and services from other European countries, in the pre-integration years. They do not recall the erstwhile controls at borders, the restrictions on movement, establishment and work in neighbouring countries, the limited amounts at their disposal when travelling abroad, the general restrictions on capital movements, the snags of dealing in several currencies, etc. Young Europeans tend even to disregard the bloody wars fought by their forefathers with nations that they themselves now consider friendly and allied with their own nation [see section 7.1.4.].

Many explanations have been advanced for the negative vote of the French and Dutch citizens at the referendums of 29 May and 1 June 2005 on the **ratification of the Constitutional Treaty**: national rather than European concerns, social protection versus free competition, fear of actual and future enlargements of the Union, etc. [see section 7.1.7]. They all have their grain of truth; but to our mind, the main cause of the negative stance of two nations that were among the original builders of the European edifice is the incomprehension of large segments of the populations of the objectives and the achievements of European integration to date.

The incomprehension of European citizens of the great experience in which they are taking part may be attributed to a communication pandemonium that ends up in an information deficit. General information on the work of European institutions is abundant and freely available to citizens for the asking, particularly in electronic form. Practically, everything that is done or discussed in the European institutions is open to the public, just for the asking [see section 7.1.5]. However, most citizens do not and never will go asking for information about an experiment that they consider as extremely complex and distant from their everyday problems and interests. Instead of expecting the citizens to seek out information themselves, European institutions and the governments of the Member States should make every effort to inform them jointly and in harmony about the objectives and the results of their European activities. Such **a common information policy is lacking in Europe** [see section 7.2.1.].

Concerning everyday information of the citizens by the mass media, there are two problems. The first is that most media rarely report the decisions of EC/EU institutions, probably because they are too technical, too detailed and often quite difficult to understand for the general public and sometimes for the journalists themselves. Instead they tend to accentuate the usual and comprehensible disagreements in the deliberations of the Council, stemming from different socioeconomic structures, cultural traditions and vested interests. Moreover, the media of a country tend to present as right the national points of view and as wrong those of the other Member States. When a compromise solution is found within the framework of the co-decision procedure of the Council and the Parliament [see section 5.2.4] and a Community measure (regulation, directive or decision) is adopted, the same media tend either to ignore it or to summarise its content in small print and in a language difficult to understand for the average citizen.

The second problem that superimposes the first is that the news about European policies, laws, programmes and internal and external activities is for most citizens like the leaves of a tree, which hide the forest that is stretching out behind them. Everyday news are uninteresting and ephemeral like the leaves in a forest - not worthy of particular attention. On the other hand, the dense forest of European institutions, policies and laws, which produces the political and economic oxygen necessary for the blossoming of small and medium European nations, is obscure and terrifying, if there is no roadmap showing its extent and the way through it.

The object of this book is to provide a roadmap of the European Union, a pathway through the maze of the European construction. The general question that pervades the whole book is **whether the European Union needs a Constitution** or, put differently, whether the EC/EU can live and develop without a Constitution (the one signed by the heads of governments of the twenty-five on 29 October 2004 or another one). There is no simple answer to this question. To answer it correctly, it is necessary to examine the whole European integration process to date: its reasons, its objectives, its governance, its stages, its achievements and its outlook. This is done in the various chapters of this book [see in particular sections 7.2.3 and 7.2.4.].

We have attempted, in this book, to assess the European integration experience as simply as possible. Details are discarded in order to facilitate the comprehension of the main elements of this - admittedly complicated - experience. Short answers are given to the main questions that both European citizens and interested people from other parts of the world may ask themselves about what is going in Europe. Technical terms and the jargon of European institutions are explained in as plain a language as possible. The book does not have to be read from end to end. The reader may choose to read only the answers to the questions that are of most interest to him or her. Cross-references link the different sections of the book, so that the reader may connect between themselves the various elements and mechanisms needed for the elements and mechanisms needed for the building and functioning of the European edifice.

The **deductions concerning the evolution of the European integration process** are set out in the final chapter, but, of course, the reader may make his or her own deductions on the basis of the partial answers to the various questions asked throughout the book. The central goal of this book is not to convince the reader about the good results of the integration process. It is to help the reader to understand this process in which he or she is participating and to think of possible ways of influencing it.

Chapter 1

THE EUROPEAN INTEGRATION PROCESS

Twenty-five centuries after the invention of democracy, Europeans made another great socio-political invention, **multinational integration**. As the first invention placed the interests of all citizens above the interests of the few powerful, so the second placed the interests of all participating nations above the interests of a few big ones. Just as the first eliminated the conflicts between different groups of citizens for power, so the second did away with the battles for the predominance of some nations over the others. Like the first, the second discovery based the peace and the prosperity of the citizens on commonly accepted institutions and laws. Just like the first, the second is constantly endangered by demagogues and oligarchs who seek to impose and ensure their own ideals and interests over the ideals and interests of the majority. The only guarantee of successful functioning of both inventions is the commitment of the majority of citizens to their structures and functions. The fortification of both democracy and multinational integration is the good information of the citizens, but this fortification can easily fall into the hands of their enemies and be used against them [see section 7.1.6].

1.1. European multinational integration

1.1.1. What is the European integration process?

European unification is based on a **multinational integration process**, defined as the voluntary establishment by treaty, concluded between independent states, of common institutions and the gradual development by them of common policies pursuing common goals and serving common interests. Being "voluntary", a multinational integration process is clearly distinguished from any form of coercive governance or coalition of nations or states. A "multinational" integration process between several nations should be distinguished from "international integration", which could one far-off day involve all or most nations of the world. It should also be distinguished from "regional integration", a concept frequently used to denote the unification of various states of a region of the world, but which should, in fact, be reserved to the economic convergence of various regions of a state, a process that is going on in most countries of the world. Multinational integration may go on inside one state containing different nationalities, but, in this case, its institutions are based on a federal constitution rather than on a treaty between independent states.

The "gradual development" of common policies implies that multinational integration is a constantly evolving process without a clearly defined end [see section 1.3.4]. Since the process is voluntary, it ensues that independent states may join it at any point, following the procedures and criteria laid down by the group, or leave it, if they consider that the common policies developed or envisaged by the majority of the members of the group do not coincide any more with their national interests.

The primary goal of multinational integration is the **achievement of peace and security** among the member states as well as between them and the rest of the world. But, unlike a military alliance where this goal is pursued by various pledges of a political and military nature, a multinational integration scheme is built gradually **by means of a large number of common policies**, cementing common interests and creating a real solidarity among the member states [see section 1.3.1].

1.1.2. Is multinational integration an economic or a political process?

Common policies, developed gradually, foster both **political and economic integration** of the participating states. Although multinational integration depends on political decisions, it greatly affects the economies of the member states. Increasingly, through the stages of customs union, common market and economic and monetary union, it opens up the participating economies to multinational trade and competition [see chapter 6]. Obviously, the economies of the member states are greatly influenced by common economic and other policies. As these economies are gradually opened up to multinational trade and competition, **all economic parameters change**: trade increases enormously within the large internal market, both supply and demand conditions are modified drastically, state intervention is seriously curbed and new dynamics are set in motion, notably concerning trade and investment opportunities. The creation and/or extension of multinational companies and the cross investments between them and national companies bind the economies of the member states closely together [see section 6.2]. The common policies build, in fact, a new concept and context of political economy, which affects the actions of political leaders and the activities of businessmen of the member states.

Indeed, by bringing about tougher conditions of competition than the ones existing inside the previously protected economies, multinational integration brings about **radical changes in business habits** and creates new business opportunities. Not surprisingly, business associations, constituting powerful interest groups, try to influence the integration process in their favour. They intervene by way of demands, suggestions or criticisms addressed to the principal actors - the common institutions and the governments of the Member States - at various stages of the decision-making process concerning particular policies or the advancement of the integration process itself, which they usually support.

As the integration process advances from the stage of the common market to that of economic and monetary union, **it spills over from the economic to the political field**. The monetary policies of the participating member states are replaced by a single policy defined and exercised by the central bank of the group of states having integrated a single currency [see section 6.3.6]. Their economic policies are closely monitored by the common institutions. Other common policies in the competition, social, fiscal, environment and other fields greatly influence national policies and restrict the freedom of movement of the governments and of the political parties that back them in the national parliaments. In its final stage, that of political union, the political aspects of the integration process become more evident, to the extent that the member states agree to define and exercise their home, judicial, external and security policies together [see section 6.4]. In return, they define and monitor, through the common institutions, the policies of their partners. In any case the political decisions of the governments of the Member States are greatly influenced by the common policies agreed by them.

The consequence of all these common policies is that the decisions taken by the common institutions have an ever increasing influence on the **professional and the everyday lives of the citizens** of the Member States. These must, therefore, participate in the decision-making process indirectly through their elected governments and their representatives at the European Parliament [see section 5.2.4]. Through them, they must be able to influence the integration process, in the same way as they influence the political life in a country. Otherwise, we have a democratic deficit at the union level [see section 5.2.5].

1.1.3. How does the multinational integration process get started?

Although they are of paramount importance, economic pressures alone cannot start the integration process. The necessary condition for setting the multinational integration process in motion is that the political, economic and other elite of neighbouring countries are earnestly seeking to **serve the interests of their nations**, rather than their own personal interests or those of a particular class or societal category. Under this condition - which implies democratic regimes - economic and political leaders would sooner or later concur that trade liberalisation better serves the supreme national goals of peace and prosperity than existing protectionist economic policies.

If they accept this standpoint, the political elite of interested nations would then have to agree among themselves which course of trade liberalisation to follow: signing a simple agreement outlining the steps to be taken to free trade among their countries or signing a treaty setting off and institutionalising a multinational integration process [see section 1.2.1]. Political parties, economic elite, media magnates and various interest groups would normally be involved in this intense debate. In democratic countries all the pros and cons of intergovernmental cooperation liberalising trade, on the one hand, and of multinational integration, on the other, would be heard and weighed. If the course of multinational integration was chosen, it would thus normally have the support of the majority of the political and economic forces in the participating countries, although the supporters of intergovernmental cooperation would not necessarily disarm and might continue advocating their points of view [see section 6.3.3].

1.2. Integration method and intergovernmental method

1.2.1. What is the difference between the integration method and the intergovernmental method of trade liberalisation?

Trade liberalisation can be obtained both by intergovernmental cooperation and by multinational integration. **Intergovernmental cooperation** is a conventional shelter of national interests, entrenched in the solid and familiar bulwark of national sovereignties defended by national governments. It does not need strong central institutions or a great deal of common legislation. Although it is usually based on a treaty, which prescribes governmental action and behaviour for the reduction of trade barriers and sanctions in case of infringement by a participating state, the respect of the agreement depends more on the goodwill of the participating governments than on common legislation enacted and enforced by supranational bodies. By signing an intergovernmental cooperation agreement for trade liberalisation, such as that of the European Free Trade Area (EFTA) [see section 2.2.1] or of the World Trade Organisation, a government pledges to curb its freedom of action in the domain of tariffs and trade, but does not shed national sovereignty in this field. In case of a serious dispute with its partners, it may free its state from its obligations without grave legal or political consequences, other than the concurrent loss of the rights provided by the agreement.

In contrast, **multinational integration** is a dynamic venture of promoting national interests, depending on many unpredictable internal and external parameters and moved forward perpetually by the ever-changing requirements of the partners and by the extra energy provided by the combination of their forces. It requires common institutions [see chapter 4] and leads progressively to the establishment of a great number of common policies, to the harmonisation of legislations and to the common management of significant parts of national sovereignties. Small and big countries participating in the process have the same rights and obligations. They pledge themselves to pursue common objectives, which go much beyond trade liberalisation. In addition to this goal, the nations participating in an integration process also want to liberalise the movements of persons and capital and to facilitate the establishment and provision of services by companies from the partner countries. The legal acts needed to achieve all these ends create strong and innumerable ties between the economies, societies and polities of the participating states [see chapter 5].

Hence, the **fundamental decision to establish a multinational integration process**, outlined in a treaty, signed and ratified by willing governments, is the catalyst, which would precipitate a sequence of secondary decisions formulating various common policies. If the implementation of these initial common policies gave satisfactory but not optimal economic results, it would reveal the necessity for more common policies and would thus have a multiplicative effect on the process [see section 1.3]. There is no predictable end to this process, as it depends on all sorts of internal and external factors. Depending on the stimuli exerted on the actors by those factors, the process may temporarily be slowed down or speeded up, but its general trend is progressive. An abrupt end to the multinational integration process is theoretically possible, but becomes increasingly improbable as the process itself continuously strengthens and multiplies the economic, political and cultural links between the participating nations.

1.2.2. Are the intergovernmental and the integration method incompatible or complementary?

The governments which opt for the integration method cannot apply it immediately in all economic sectors, let alone in non-economic fields. The integration process being evolutionary, they have to proceed step by step and apply the integration or Community method, firstly, to the abolition of the most important obstacles hindering the economic relations of their states. As they solve this first series of problems they come across a multitude of lesser problems, which also require solution in view of the efficient functioning of their markets. Since the solutions to arising problems have to be agreed by all or at least the vast majority of participants and since the conciliation of the various interests involved requires many years of negotiations, the integration process is necessarily slow. Until an optimal solution to a particular problem is found by the Community method, the actors of the integration process have to resort to intergovernmental cooperation, in order to set common objectives, compare best practices to achieve them and, in any case, avoid widening the gaps between their policies on the matter. It ensues that, in the integration process, all economic policies and a growing number of non-economic ones are made up partly of common policy measures and partly of intergovernmental cooperation measures, the main difference between them being that the first have mandatory effects whereas the latter do not [see section 5.3].

As common policies necessitate transfers of national sovereignties to the shared sovereignty, they have to be agreed by all the participants and outlined in the treaty. The treaty may also set objectives that should be pursued by intergovernmental cooperation; but such objectives may also be defined by the common institutions in the normal course of their work. The measures taken to pursue such objectives serve the learning process and usually pave the way for common policies formulated and managed by the Community method. These policies have again to be outlined in the treaty and, therefore, the treaty needs to be amended from time to time to set the ever higher objectives of integration.

It follows from what precedes that the intergovernmental method and the Community method are complementary, but that the latter tends to replace the former in a growing number of areas as the integration process marches forward. The reverse cannot happen, since intergovernmental cooperation does not have the institutions necessary to manage the Community method. The members of an intergovernmental cooperation scheme (e.g. the European Free Trade Area) [see section 2.2.1], may, however, in the framework of a broad cooperation/integration scheme (such as the European Economic Area) [see section 2.2.3], adapt to their needs some legal and financial instruments developed and managed by the institutions of an integration scheme (i.e. those of the European Community/Union).

1.3. The development of common policies

Multinational integration is based on common policies, which develop and multiply thanks to the Community decision-making procedure or the Community method that characterizes it [see section 5.2.1]. Hence, common policies are the essential elements of a multinational integration process.

1.3.1. What is the definition of a common policy?

A common policy, as far as multinational integration is concerned, is defined as a set of rules, codes of conduct, decisions and measures adopted by the common institutions set up by a group of states and implemented by the common institutions and the member states. A real common policy (to be distinguished from a so-called one) has to be implemented by all the participants and, therefore, needs to be monitored by supranational executive and judiciary authorities. Hence, by adopting a common policy, the participants agree to transfer some of their sovereign powers to common supranational institutions [see section 3.3.2].

This **transfer of sovereign rights** in the framework of common policies is the main drawback but also the fundamental characteristic of multinational integration. It explains why common policies are difficult to adopt, but also why, once adopted, they are the binding (or integrating) elements of the whole multinational structure. Common policies, thus, distinguish multinational integration from intergovernmental cooperation and explain nationalistic scepticism towards the former [see section 2.1.2].

1.3.2. Are there various types of common policies?

There are **four main types** of common policies: fundamental and secondary, horizontal and sectoral. The **fundamental** ones could also be called framework common policies, because their basic objectives and scope are inscribed in the treaty itself and need, therefore, to be agreed by all the participants. **Secondary** common policies are the ones that are defined by the common legislative bodies within the framework of the fundamental common policies and in accordance with the Community decision-making process [see section 5.2.1]. Both fundamental and secondary common policies can be divided into **horizontal** (such as social, competition or environment protection), which affect the overall conditions of the economies and societies of the member states and **sectoral**, which concern certain sectors of the economies of the member states (namely industry, energy, transports, agriculture and fisheries). All common policies can be classified in a decreasing order of importance, depending on the scope of the area covered by each one.

Multinational integration itself is, in fact, the most important fundamental common policy, since it is initially chosen by a number of states in preference to isolationism or intergovernmental cooperation [see section 1.2.1]. Integration is, indeed, the fundamental course of action (the trunk), decided voluntarily, in common, in a treaty, from which all other common policies depend or emanate (like the branches of a tree). As the integration process develops in stages, the passage from one stage to the next - from customs union to common market, then to economic and monetary union and finally to political union - is also based on a **fundamental common policy** decision inscribed in a treaty [see section 3.2]. These common policies, which frame the stages of the integration process, are the most important ones - the thicker branches of the tree.

From them stem thinner branches concerning less important fundamental policies also framed in the treaty, for instance on competition, environment protection or agriculture. From such fundamental policies emanate ever finer **secondary policies**, which are laid down by the common institutions and are implemented by them and the member states. For environment protection, for instance, there needs to be a general policy for the protection of the atmosphere and then specific measures defined in regulations, directives or decisions. Such measures may be classified as specific common policies.

1.3.3. How do common policies materialise?

Common policies materialise when, where and to the extent that the governments, representing the parties to an integration treaty, believe that the individual interests of their states are better served by them than by national policies. To create a sentiment of mutual confidence, the formulation of a common policy by the common institutions must clearly indicate the **common need** that it addresses, the **common goal(s)** that it pursues and the **common interest** that it serves. The essential element in a common policy is the definition of the common interest in the objectives and measures framed by it [see section 5.2.3]. This definition has to satisfy all member states as far as fundamental common policies are concerned and most member states concerning secondary common policies [see section 5.2.6].

It is normal that some common policies better satisfy the national interests of some participants than those of others. It is abnormal and impracticable that all common policies better satisfy the interests of some members of the group to the detriment of the rest. Indeed, no party to a multinational integration scheme should feel that its national interests are being permanently and systematically injured by the common policies proposed; but, on the other hand, no party to such a scheme may systematically obstruct the common policies proposed, by claiming that they do not fully satisfy its national interests. Hence, all parties to a multinational integration scheme must be prepared to accept compromise solutions formulated in the various common policies discussed at a certain point of time and, sometimes, to give ground in one field, expecting to gain ground in another field [see section 5.1.1]. The hundreds of decisions taken every year by the EC/EU institutions demonstrate the fact that its members play the game according to this rule. The few exceptions confirm the rule.

1.3.4. How do common policies develop?

If the participants play the game according to the rules set by them in the treaty, they would tend to develop and multiply common policies according to their ever-changing needs. This happens because common policies, like all other public policies, are there to answer the needs which arise in a particular community at a particular time. These needs change and multiply over time. Therefore, not only the objectives that the member states set for each common policy, but also the means that they give to the common institutions to attain them and the measures that the latter adopt in order to implement them have to keep pace with the new and changing economic, political and social needs of the states, participating in the integration process.

A common policy may develop in two senses: in the sense of its legal evolution, which is required in order to keep up with economic and technical progress in the subject matter that it covers; and in the sense of the expansion of its field, which may happen in order to cover peripheral needs not formerly attended to in the formulation of the policy or new needs, either encountered during the implementation of the measures originally adopted or created by the geopolitical environment of the moment. Moreover, a common policy tends to spill over into the areas of other common policies, produce needs, cause reactions and nourish their development. Thus, common policies are closely knit together, support each other, foster their joint evolution and multiplication and, in so doing, promote the progress of the multinational integration process [see section 6.2.8].

Chapter 2

BIRTH AND GROWTH OF THE EUROPEAN COMMUNITY/UNION

In 1945, just after the Second World War, **Winston Churchill** described Europe as "a rubble heap, a charnel house, a breeding ground for pestilence and hate". A year later, on 19 September 1946, in his famous Zurich speech, he proposed as a remedy "to recreate the European Family ... and to provide it with a structure under which it can dwell in peace, in safety and in freedom ... a kind of United States of Europe". Half a century later, realising and exceeding Churchill's vision, the western part (and recently the central part) of the "European Family" had become an island of peace and prosperity in a world ravaged by hatreds, conflicts, civil wars and misery. The successful formula that European nations had invented to overcome their depression was the integration of the formerly antagonistic nation-states into a union of peacefully interacting and competing nations. The **multinational integration formula** involves the gradual creation of imperceptible albeit innumerable links between the nations taking part in the process. Those links consist of common policies and common laws, which govern the Member States' economic activities and influence the day-to-day lives and occupations of their citizens. The integration formula may some day lead to Churchill's vision of a "United States of Europe", but then it would be replaced by a federation formula and a complete reform of the common institutions of the participating states [see section 7.2.8].

2.1. The original Six

The march of European unification began with six countries, pioneers starting out on an unknown road. Some European states did not want and some could not participate in the march. Some states advocated another way forward [see section 2.2.1]. Others stood by as spectators and joined the march when they ascertained that it was going along the right path. Finally, after half a century of continuous progress, all European nations are following or want to follow the common march, even if some are dragging their feet and trying to check the speed of the vanguard [see section 2.2.2].

2.1.1. What motivated European unification?

World War II had left Europe clearly divided into **two very distinct groups of states**. In the East, the Soviet Union with Russian land and population supremacy and with a unifying ideology appealing to impoverished people could annex its neighbouring countries and install friendly regimes. Moreover, it could offer them a kind of security (although under totalitarian regimes), a large market for their imports and exports (although under Russian domination) and a certain safeguard for the most basic interests of their populations - food and shelter. In Western Europe, in the 1950s, the welfare of the populations was not much better than that in Central and Eastern Europe. Although in most Western European countries people lived under democratic regimes and could enjoy some fundamental human rights, the economic situation of the vast majority was not much better than that of their Eastern neighbours. Moreover, their fragile democratic regimes were at threat both from outside - the arrogant superpower that was quickly becoming the Soviet Union - and from inside - the political parties friendly to it.

Was this threat the prime stimulus for European unification? It certainly was a reason for cooperation, but not the primary factor. To face the Soviet threat, most Western European nations had placed themselves, already since 1949, inside the North Atlantic Treaty Organisation (NATO) and hence under the American nuclear umbrella. This umbrella could be a much better deterrent from outside menace than a unification of their inadequate armies. But, this umbrella could not safeguard the **fragile democratic regimes** from the unrest of people living under subsistence levels. To curb this threat, the stagnating economies of Western European countries would have to be revamped to absorb the jobless and penniless populations.

These economies were separated from each other and from the rest of the world by high tariff and other barriers, which allowed some inefficient public and private companies to survive in the **protected national market**, but effectively excluded foreign trade and competition and, hence, the expansion that they could provide. To stimulate the development of Western European economies, the barriers between them had to be torn down. But, again, the stimulus of trade liberalisation was not enough in itself to start European unification. A political decision was needed to pursue this liberalisation by multinational integration rather than by intergovernmental cooperation.

2.1.2. Why did some countries prefer integration to cooperation?

The simple way to trade liberalisation in Europe was the creation of a **free trade area** through intergovernmental cooperation. This course was advocated mainly by the United Kingdom and the Scandinavian countries [see section 2.2.1]. According to this view, trade liberalisation in Western Europe could accelerate and exceed the work begun in 1947 at international level by the General Agreement on Tariffs and Trade (GATT). It could thus lead to total abolition of tariff barriers, without any concession of national sovereignty. In parallel, an intergovernmental cooperation for economic development, without legal obligations, could be pursued between Western European nations and the United States of America inside the European Organisation for Economic Cooperation. This organisation was established in the 1950s in order to manage the Marshall Plan of the USA for the reconstruction of Europe and was later transformed into the actual Organisation for Economic Cooperation and Development (OECD), which includes most European countries, the USA and other Anglo-Saxon countries.

But some politicians in continental countries, which had been devastated by the wars between themselves, wanted to go beyond trade liberalisation. They wanted to tie their economies so close together as **to make a new civil war in Europe impossible**. They wanted to try a method which would combine trade liberalisation with economic integration. As the word integration implies, they wanted to unify their separated economies into a whole. Multinational integration was, at the time, a revolutionary and risky enterprise. It was revolutionary, because it clashed with the well established concept of the nation-state and the national sovereignty that emanated from it. It was a risky enterprise, because it required the setting up of supranational institutions that would prevail over national authorities with unknown consequences. However, it promised to transform the former enemies into partners and, moreover, to make their partnership irrevocable. Six States were ready to take the plunge: France, Germany, Italy, the Netherlands, Belgium and Luxembourg. But, they did not want to gamble all their economies. They decided, first, to bet on their coal and steel sectors.

2.1.3. What was the European Coal and Steel Community?

The European Coal and Steel Community (ECSC) was designed as a test for European integration. The coal and steel industries were, in the 1950s, the core of the industrial sectors of the original Member States. The combination of coal, the major energy at the time, with steel, the prime industrial product of the Ruhr valley, had built the might of the Third Reich and helped it to conquer almost all of continental Europe. In post-war Europe, these industries were composed of a few large companies, which were often subsidised, protected from international competition by high tariff and other barriers and were allowed to conclude among themselves agreements leading to national cartels. If these industries were put together in a multinational project managed by supranational authorities, Germany could, from a potential enemy, become a partner with its neighbouring countries. By participating in a scheme, which would control its war industries, Germany would pledge not simply by words but by deeds that it had abandoned forever any intentions of expanding its "Lebensraum". Moreover, if economic integration could work in these highly protected industries, it could work in other sectors.

This, in a nutshell, was the brilliant idea of **Jean Monnet**, inspired by his business and political activities with the Allies during the war. It was proclaimed by the French Minister of Foreign Affairs, **Robert Schuman**, on 9 May 1950, a historical date for European unification, recognised as such by the Constitutional Treaty. The Schuman declaration was quite explicit on the road to be followed by European integration: "Europe will not be made all at once, or according to a single plan. It will be built through concrete achievements which first create a de facto solidarity." The ECSC was to be the first achievement. The French idea was immediately welcomed by the German Chancellor, Konrad Adenauer, and by the Prime Ministers of Italy, Belgium, the Netherlands and Luxembourg. Less than a year after the Schuman declaration the founding fathers had negotiated the details of this novel project and were able to sign the ECSC Treaty, in Paris, on 18 April 1951 [see section 3.1.1]. The institutions that they set up at that time - a High Authority (integrated in 1967 into the European Commission), a Council of Ministers, a European Assembly (which developed into the European Parliament) and a Court of Justice - are still there today, with, of course, extended functions. The durability of the institutions demonstrates how well the original project was designed.

In fact, the avowed intentions of the founders of the ECSC were that this Community should be an experiment, which could gradually be extended to other economic sectors. For this reason, the duration of the ECSC Treaty was limited to fifty years. On 23 July 2002, when this period expired, the specific rules concerning the coal and steel sectors were integrated in the overall European Community policies and legislation. In fact, the ECSC experiment had proved to be successful already in the first ten years of its existence and had led to the creation of the European Economic Community.

2.1.4. What was the European Economic Community?

The very first years of the functioning of the common market in coal and steel showed that economic integration was possible and worthwhile and that it could be extended to all products. Thus, already in June 1955, the Six started discussing the possibility of creating a common market embracing all the sectors of their economies. Less than two years later, on 25 March 1957, a record time considering the vastness of the project, the Six were able to sign, on Capitol Hill in Rome, the Treaties establishing the European Economic Community (EEC) and the European Atomic Energy Community (EAEC). This last Community, which oversees the production of nuclear energy for peaceful purposes, is still in existence. On the contrary, the European Economic Community, which established and managed an early customs union and common market, does not exist anymore, since it was transformed in 1991, by the Treaty of Maastricht, into the broader European Community (EC) [see sections 3.1.2 and 3.2.1 to 3.3.3].

2.1.5. What is the European Atomic Energy Community?

The Treaty establishing the **European Atomic Energy Community (EAEC**, but more commonly known as **Euratom**) was also signed in Rome on 25 March 1957 and came into force on 1 January 1958. Its aim was to create a common market for nuclear materials and equipment, establish common nuclear legislation, introduce a common system for supplies of fissile materials and establish a system for supervising the peaceful use of nuclear energy and common standards for nuclear safety and for the health and safety protection of the population and workers against ionising radiation. The key elements in this Treaty were, however, the coordination of the research programmes of the Member States and a joint research programme, implemented in a Joint Research Centre, which was to develop technology and stimulate nuclear production in Europe.

Although it was very much in the spotlight at the time of its establishment, Euratom has experienced many ups and downs as a result both of disillusionment as regards nuclear energy's economic prospects and of the ambition of some Member States to develop their own nuclear industry (and not purely for civil purposes). Nevertheless, the EAEC Treaty is still in force and manages quite well the nuclear energy sector of the Community/Union. The Euratom Supply Agency has the exclusive right to conclude contracts for the supply of ores, source materials and special fissile materials originating inside or outside the Community. The Euratom Safeguards Office has the task of ensuring that nuclear material is not diverted from its intended use within the European Union and that the Member States comply with the Community's safeguards obligations.

2.2. How the Six became Twenty-five

During the 1960s and the 1970s, the three original Communities (ECSC, EEC, EAEC) achieved a great deal. They boosted intra-Community trade spectacularly, they invigorated competition, they encouraged the modernisation of industry, agriculture and the services, they bolstered economic development and particularly that of the least developed regions, they favoured employment thanks to the free movement of workers and, in general, they raised significantly the welfare of the nations participating in the integration scheme. In addition to these economic achievements, nations not participating in the experiment were surprised to see the former enemies become increasingly good partners and friends. They, thus, understood that the experiment was not only economic but also political and that, consequently, the European Economic Community could offer something more than the European Free Trade Area.

2.2.1. What is the European Free Trade Area?

While the Six started experimenting with economic integration in the 1950s, the United Kingdom and some other countries favoured the intergovernmental method of liberalising trade, which did not involve transfers of national sovereignty [see section 1.2.1]. The intergovernmental cooperation for trade liberalisation took shape in 1959 with the creation of the **European Free Trade Association (EFTA)**, to which the United Kingdom, Norway, Sweden, Denmark, Austria, Portugal, Iceland and Switzerland acceded, with Finland joining at a later date. But this impressive original membership of the EFTA was soon to dwindle through defections to the EEC camp. Defections were led by the leader of the group, the United Kingdom, which already two years after the creation of the EFTA declared its wish to switch camps. After a decade of hard negotiations and two resounding "non" by the French President, General de Gaulle, the UK acceded to the EEC, in 1973, along with Denmark and Ireland. Twelve years later, in 1995, three more members of EFTA, Austria, Sweden and Finland acceded to the EC/EU, so that, now, the only members of EFTA are Switzerland, Norway, Iceland and the tiny Liechtenstein.

The government of Norway applied twice for EEC membership and even signed the accession treaty, in 1972 and in 1992, but this accession was twice turned down by a slight majority of the Norwegian people, which rightly or wrongly feared that integration would threaten national interests in two important sectors, oil production and fisheries. The political elite of Switzerland have often flirted with the idea of EC/EU membership, but have been put off by the negative stance of the population, led by isolationist mass media.

2.2.2. How did the European Community/Union's membership grow?

With the accessions of the **United Kingdom, Ireland and Denmark**, on 1 January 1973, the members of the EEC became nine. Once democracy was restored in Greece, Portugal and Spain, these countries submitted applications for accession to the European Community. These countries thus chose to join the novel and hence risky experiment of the EEC rather than the secure but limited refuge of the EFTA. They considered that multinational integration could not only better promote their economic development, but would also uphold their frail democratic regimes, since its institutions require democratic institutions in the participating countries. Greece acceded to the European Community on 1 January 1981, and Spain and Portugal on 1 January 1986. Thus, for a brief moment in its history, the EEC was known as "the Twelve".

But, on 1 January 1995, the Europe of Twelve became the Europe of Fifteen, with the accession of **Austria, Finland and Sweden**. These three nations had weighed the economic advantages of European integration against the political disadvantage of a loss of some sovereign rights and had decided to take the train of integration despite the cost of the fare. Norway, as seen above, stayed at the platform.

After the fall of the iron curtain in 1989, one after the other the countries of Central and Eastern Europe applied for membership to the EU, thus clearly opting for multinational integration rather than for intergovernmental cooperation inside EFTA [see section 2.2.1]. Their preference was guided both by expectations of faster economic development and by hopes of increased political stability inside a Union of democratic countries. The former satellites of the Soviet Union decided, in fact, to trade some of their newly acquired national sovereignty for the strength promised by the shared sovereignty of the Union. The EU encouraged their application by political and financial means and started accession negotiations with **Poland, Hungary, the Czech Republic, Slovakia, Slovenia, Estonia, Latvia, Lithuania** plus **Cyprus and Malta**. After conclusion of the negotiations, these ten countries signed the Treaty of Accession in Athens on 16 April 2003 and have been full members of the EC/EU since 1 May 2004. We, therefore, now speak of the Union of Twenty five.

2.2.3. What is the European Economic Area?

Despite their differing views as to the method of trade liberalisation, the economic and political relations between the EC/EU and European Free Trade Area (EFTA) were always excellent and are becoming ever closer [see section 2.2.1]. Free trade agreements were signed in 1972 and 1973 between the Community and the EFTA countries. These agreements abolished customs duties and restrictions on trade in industrial products and organised trade in agricultural products. These arrangements have operated in a satisfactory manner and have brought about sustained growth in trade between the two groups of countries.

When the EEC undertook to complete its single market by 1992, it offered to the EFTA to further strengthen the relations between the two trading blocs. The Treaty on the **European Economic Area (EEA)** was signed in 1992 by the governments of twelve EU countries and six EFTA countries. However, as a result of the negative Swiss referendum on the EEA Treaty, and the accession to the European Union since 1 January 1995 of the former EFTA members Austria, Sweden and Finland, the EEA Treaty associates to the **EC/EU** only **Norway, Iceland and Liechtenstein**. The new members of the EU have acceded to the EEA, which thus numbers 28 countries.

The EEA-EFTA States undertook to take on board existing Community legislation concerning the free movement of goods, persons, services and capital, subject to a few exceptions. On top of the **implementation of the "four freedoms" of the common market** [see section 6.2.2], the EEA Agreement provides for close relations between the Community and the EFTA countries in areas which have an impact on business activity, notably social policy, consumer protection, environment, statistics and company law, research and development, information, education, the audiovisual sector, SMEs and tourism. In fact, the EFTA countries (including Switzerland in some respects) participate practically in the common market without participating in the decision making process that governs it, but by adapting its legislation to their circumstances.

2.3. The attractive force of the Union

2.3.1. What does the growing membership of the EC/EU show?

The growing membership of the Community/Union demonstrates the **extraordinary attractiveness of the multinational integration process**, using the Community method, compared to its rival, the intergovernmental cooperation method [see section 1.2.1]. The countries, which had originally advocated the latter method, have come, one after the other, to solicit their participation in the integration process [see section 2.2.2]. The countries of Western Europe, which still shy away from this process, are nevertheless following many of the policies decided by the countries participating in the process, thanks to the European Economic Area (EEA) agreement [see section 2.2.1]. The countries of Central and Eastern Europe, which, after their liberation from the iron curtain, had the option of joining the outer circle of the free trade EFTA/EEA or the inner circle of the EC/EU, have unhesitatingly opted for the latter. The facts speak for themselves. There could be no better demonstration of the validity of the multinational integration (Community) method than the attraction that it exerts on outsider neighbouring countries.

What is even more extraordinary is that the membership has kept growing together with the tasks assumed by the team, which means that the newcomers accede to an ever closer union and undertake to adopt all the "acquis communautaire", i.e. all the ever-growing legislation enacted by the institutions set up by the elder members [see chapter 5]. Earlier accessions happened at the time that the Community had just realised its customs union and was struggling to complete its common market in order to make it a single market [see chapter 6.2]. The newcomers could well believe that the integration process would stop at this stage and, in fact, some still wish that it had and feel betrayed that it marches on and on. But, later day accessions happened at times that the Community/Union had declared, in revised Treaties, its intention to proceed to the stages of economic and monetary union and even to political union [see section 3.2]. Hence, when they signed and ratified these Treaties, they were fully aware that European integration is a process without a specified end, but with the declared objective of bringing the European peoples ever closer together. This means that recent newcomers and applicants are attracted by the economic and political advantages of integration, which, for them, outweigh the disadvantage of conferring parts of their national sovereignties to supranational institutions [see section 1.2.1].

2.3.2. How far can the Union expand?

The attraction continues and it seems likely that all the countries in the periphery of the Union will someday ask for accession to it. The accession negotiations with Romania and Bulgaria are quite advanced and these countries are expected to accede in 2007 or 2008. In December 2004, the EU accepted to start accession negotiations with Croatia and Turkey. As soon as their economic and political situation allows, all Balkan countries are expected to seek a safe haven inside the Union, which, in the next decade, could thus number more than thirty members.

On its side, the Union does not seem disposed to close its door. The **Constitutional Treaty** [see section 3.3] declares that the Union shall be open to all European States which respect its values and are committed to promoting them together (Art. I-1). These values are: human dignity, freedom, democracy, equality, the rule of law, respect for human rights, including the rights of persons belonging to minorities, pluralism, non-discrimination, tolerance, justice, solidarity and equality between women and men (Art. I-2).

All this is very well, but there is a problem of definition of the concepts "**European States**" and "**respect its values**". These concepts may be defined either in a narrow or a broad sense. Who will define them? The European institutions (Commission, Parliament, Council) or the peoples of the Union through referendums? And, if the latter are asked to give their opinion, by whom and how will they be adequately informed in order to be able to express themselves on such difficult subjects [see section 7.1.7]? It is not up to us to answer such questions or those that depend on them, such as: are Turkey, Russia or the Ukraine European states and do they respect the values of the Union? And, if yes, should they be admitted to the Union if they ask for their accession? It is up to the political leaders of the Union to take a courageous stance on these questions. They cannot expect the peoples of the Union to answer questions, which they themselves fail to tackle before they make the major decisions on the future of Europe [see section 7.2.1].

Furthermore, the problem is not so much the continuous enlargement of the Union as that **its actual structures and institu-**

tions cannot support its expansion without their reinforcement. The signing of the Constitutional Treaty was an initial endeavour to strengthen the structures and institutions of the Union [see section 3.3]. But, it seems that the majority of citizens in some of the twenty-five nations believe that this effort is not sufficient for the further enlargement of the Union, whereas the majorities in other nations believe quite the opposite: that this strengthening should be avoided in order to discourage the progress of the integration process. In other words, some nations would like a stronger Constitutional Treaty, which would not only allow further enlargements but also help the Union to stand up in the international arena and differentiate itself from other existing and developing superpowers [see section 7.2.6], particularly concerning the social protection of citizens. On the contrary, other nations would like to see the abolition of the Treaty on the European Union and the solitary existence of the Treaty on the European Community, restraining further integration and conferral of national sovereignties [see section 1.2.1]. To better understand the argumentation of the two sides, we should know what these various Treaties stand for.

Chapter 3

THE EUROPEAN TREATIES

The treaties are the primary source of European law and hence the legal basis of common policies. The states participating in a multinational integration process set in a treaty the objectives that they wish to attain, the common policies that they wish to implement in order to achieve their goals, the structure and functions of the common institutions that will enact and monitor the common legislation formulated in the framework of the common policies and the fields reserved for the cooperation of their governments [see section 1.2.2]. Since common policies need to develop and multiply in order to serve better the ever changing needs and interests of the participating states [see section 1.3.4], the treaty, which outlines them, needs also to be modified, so as to allow these states to attain the higher goals that they set. This is the pattern followed by the European Treaties.

3.1. The original Treaties

3.1.1. What were the objectives of the European Coal and Steel Community Treaty?

In his declaration of 9 May 1950, Robert Schuman, the French Minister for Foreign Affairs, proposed the creation of a **common market in two important economic sectors** which had until then been used for military purposes, namely the coal and steel sectors: it would be a matter of integrating Germany economically and politically into a European Coal and Steel Community with France and other willing countries. The sectors of coal and steel were chosen as a paradigm of European integration for both economic and political reasons [see section 2.1.3].

The Treaty establishing the **European Coal and Steel Community (ECSC)** was signed in Paris on 18 April 1951 by France, Germany, Italy, the Netherlands, Belgium and Luxembourg. Its main objective was to eliminate the various barriers to trade and to create a common market in which coal and steel products from the Member States could move freely. Capital and workers in both sectors should also circulate freely. In order that all this could be achieved, the Treaty laid down certain rules on investment, on government intervention, on agreements and concentrations, on production and prices. These rules were to be implemented by Community institutions, which would exercise the powers previously held by the states in those sectors: namely a High Authority and a special Council (of Ministers), the decisions of which would be binding on all Member States. Ambitious despite its restricted scope, the ECSC Treaty instituted a European Assembly and a European Court of Justice. These common rules and institutions signified that the cooperation of the Member States in the coal and steel sectors should be much closer than that obtained with a traditional intergovernmental cooperation [see section 1.2.1].

The ECSC Treaty effectively created and administered the common market of coal and steel. Thanks to this Treaty, import and export taxes, taxes having equivalent effect, and quantitative restrictions on product movement were abolished. The Paris Treaty laid down rules for agreements, company concentrations and dominant positions, and prohibited unfair competitive practices and discriminatory practices, i.e. the application by a seller of dissimilar conditions to comparable transactions and especially on the grounds of the nationality of the buyer. It thus succeeded to ensure that users have equal access to sources of production and to promote the development of international trade. These trade and competition rules were applied successfully for fifty years, the duration of the ECSC Treaty. Following the expiry of this Treaty on 23 July 2002, the procedural rules and secondary legislation derived from it in the two sectors have been incorporated in the general provisions of the European Community Treaty.

3.1.2. What were the objectives of the Treaty establishing the European Economic Community?

The functioning of the customs union of coal and steel immediately showed that the ECSC model could work and be extended to all economic sectors [see section 2.1.4]. Already in June 1955, the Ministers for Foreign Affairs of the Six discussed the possibility of creating a common market embracing all products and a separate Community for nuclear energy. Speedy negotiations conducted by the Belgian Minister for Foreign Affairs, Paul-Henri Spaak, were concluded in April 1956 and on 25 March 1957, the Six were able to sign, on Capitol Hill in Rome, the Treaties establishing the European Economic Community (EEC) and the European Atomic Energy Community (EAEC).

Although the EEC and EAEC treaties are sometimes referred to as the "Treaties of Rome", the "Treaty of Rome" is obviously the EEC Treaty. The essential task, which the Treaty of Rome assigned to the Community institutions, was **the creation of a common market** between the Member States. That involved: (a) the achievement of a customs union entailing, on the one hand, the abolition of customs duties, import quotas and other barriers to trade between Member States and, on the other hand, the introduction of a Common Customs Tariff (CCT) vis-à-vis third countries [see section 6.1]; and (b) the implementation, *inter alia* through common policies, of **four fundamental freedoms**: freedom of movement of goods, of course, but also freedom of movement of salaried workers, freedom of establishment and freedom to provide services by independent persons and companies and, finally, freedom of capital movements [see section 6.2].

Even though in the preamble to the Treaty the Member States declared that they were determined to lay the foundations of an ever closer union among the peoples of Europe, the Treaty itself constituted the charter for a common market, not of an economic and monetary union and certainly not of a political union. Even if the political leaders of the time had such visions, they did not spell them out in the EEC Treaty. This fact should be borne in mind by some people who claim that the dreams of the fathers of the Community/Union were not realised. However, through its Article 235 (Art. 308 TEC), the EEC Treaty gave Member States **the possibility to act in the fields not provided by it** by taking unanimously the measures required to attain one of its objectives. This allowed the Member States to implement a large number of common or, so called, Community policies without amending the Treaty [see section 1.3.1].

Nevertheless, the EEC Treaty had its limitations, the most important of which was that, although it had set a timetable for the abolition of customs barriers to trade, it had not done the same for the removal of trade barriers of equivalent effect. Used to protectionist practices, the administrations of the Member States, even after the realisation of the customs union, in July 1968, still tried to protect their inefficient national industries and companies from cross-border trade and competition, thus impeding the functioning of an effective common market. In 1985, however, the President of the European Commission, **Jacques Delors**, forcefully declared that in order to achieve the main objective of the EEC Treaty, the creation of a single market, all internal European borders should be eliminated by the end of 1992. Delors idea was taken up by the European Council and led to the signature, in June 1987, of an important amendment of the EEC, the so-called **European Single Act**. This Act, not only succeeded in removing the technical barriers to trade, thus creating the Single Market [see section 6.2.3], but also gave fresh momentum to many common policies, such as transports, taxation and environment protection.

3.2. The subsequent Treaties

3.2.1. What were the new objectives set by the Treaty of Maastricht?

As the abolition of customs barriers to trade, in 1968, had highlighted the technical and administrative obstacles to intra-Community trade, so the effort to abolish the latter, by 1992 [see section 6.2.3], made clear that the completion of the common market would not bring about a real single market as long as there were still monetary obstacles in the way. Therefore, the integrationists in the original six Member States were, already before the completion of the single market, pushing their new partners to step into the **next integration stage, that of economic and monetary union,** and even to sketch the final stage, that of political union. The defenders of the intergovernmental method were, however, reticent. They had joined the Community in order to reap the benefits of the single market and had accepted the conferrals of sovereignty necessary to that end. But they were unwilling to make any more concessions to the Community method of integration and its evolutionary properties [see section 6.3.3].

The compromise solution found in Maastricht, in December 1991, was to split the integration venture into two. The original European Economic Community Treaty was renamed **Treaty on the European Community** to signify that it set new objectives over and above the original economic ones, notably for monetary and social integration. The United Kingdom was allowed to opt out of these new goals and the people of Denmark, consulted by referendum, decided not to join the monetary union. A new **Treaty on the European Union** was signed at the same time to outline the objectives of political union, in particular those of a judicial and home affairs policy and those of a common foreign and security policy. But, by common agreement, it was decided that these goals would be pursued by intergovernmental cooperation and not by the Community method [see section 1.2.1].

Hence, the so-called Treaty of Maastricht, which was signed on 7 February 1992, was in fact **made up of two separate but interrelated Treaties**: the Treaty establishing the European Community (**TEC**), where the Community method prevailed and the Treaty on the European Union (**TEU**), which was run by intergovernmental cooperation. These two Treaties separated the European construction into three pillars or wings, distinguished mainly on the basis of the decision-making process: the main pillar or edifice, which is the European Community and where the common work of the participants is regulated by the TEC and where the Community method prevails [see section 5.2.1]; the pillar or wing of justice and home affairs; and the pillar or wing of the common foreign and security policy (CFSP) [see section 6.4]. The method of construction of the two new pillars or wings was based on intergovernmental cooperation, given that the TEU required unanimity for decision-making and, hence, any Member State could veto a common action or could disengage itself from any decision or common position without any consequences.

In any case, the Treaty of Maastricht fixed several new objectives and therefore instituted or reinforced the corresponding common policies. Through its Community wing it strengthened the policies related to the free movement of goods, persons and capital and it instituted new policies, such as economic and monetary policy, education and youth, culture, consumer protection and social protection (from which the United Kingdom was excluded by a so-called "Social Protocol"). Through the Union wing of the Maastricht Treaty, the Member States declared their intention to develop close cooperation on justice and home affairs and to assert the identity of the Union on the international stage, in particular through the implementation of a common foreign and security policy including the eventual framing of a common defence policy. However, the Union was to pursue these goals through the ineffectual intergovernmental cooperation method.

Thus, since the implementation of the Treaty of Maastricht in 1992, the European Union accompanies and complements the European Community; but since the Treaty on the latter governs a far greater number of activities and much more effectively than the Treaty on the European Union, it is more exact to speak of the **European Community/Union (EC/EU)**, in order to keep in mind that they are two different organisations and legal entities. In fact, for the time being, only the European Community has a legal personality, whereas the European Union has no legal personality at all and can therefore not sign treaties or other international legal instruments. The Constitutional Treaty was intending to correct this peculiar situation by conferring legal personality to the European Union [see section 3.3.4].

3.2.2. What were the new objectives set by the Treaty of Amsterdam?

The Treaty signed on 17 June 1997 in Amsterdam, only six years and a half after the signature of the Treaty of Maastricht, did not bring fundamental changes to the integration process, but it marked some progress in several policy areas. The most important development was the transfer under the European Community's wing, thus entailing the Community decision-making process [see section 5.2.1], of policies related to the free movement of persons, notably concerning visas, asylum and immigration (previously placed in the European Union wing). Another important objective of the Amsterdam Treaty was to place employment and **social protection** at the heart of the Union. While confirming that the Member States bear primary responsibility for employment, the revised Treaty on the European Community engaged them to act together to find solutions to unemployment. The Labour government of the United Kingdom accepted the social objectives of the EC Treaty and therefore the social policy agreement, exempting the UK from this common policy, was abolished.

Under its European Union wing, the Amsterdam Treaty strengthened somewhat the common foreign and security policy by making the European Council (heads of State or government) responsible for defining common strategies to be implemented by the Union and the Member States and by designating a High Representative for the CFSP (the Secretary General of the Council) and a Policy Planning and Early Warning Unit under his responsibility [see section 6.4.6].

3.2.3. What were the new objectives set by the Treaty of Nice?

The Treaty that was signed in Nice on 26 February 2001, only three years and a half after the signature of the Treaty of Amsterdam, did not aspire to give a fresh impetus to the European integration process, but only to prepare the institutions of the European Community/Union to function with the representatives of **ten new Member States** [see section 2.2.2]. The Treaty of Nice, which came in force on 1 February 2003 and which will stay in force until replaced by the Constitutional or another treaty [see section 7.2.4], is again composed of the Treaties on the European Union (TEU) and the Treaty establishing the European Community (TEC).

The Treaty of Nice's main revisions of the Treaty of Amsterdam concerned **institutional matters related to decision-making procedures**. It extended the qualified majority voting to new subjects, thereby boosting the role of the European Parliament in the codecision procedure with the Council [see section 5.2.4]. It reinforced and facilitated the enhanced cooperation of some Member States, in cases where an agreement cannot be reached by normal decision-making procedures [see section 5.2.7]. The Protocol on the enlargement of the European Union adopted at Nice redefined the weighting of the votes of each Member State in the Council and introduced a population element by specifying that decisions taken by qualified majority on the basis of a Commission proposal should gather at least 72% of the total votes of the members, representing at least 62% of the total population of the Union [see section 5.2.6].

3.3. The Constitutional Treaty

The coming into force of the Treaty of Nice was just a small step in the process of constant reform of the Union. Convinced of the need for a substantial revision of the institutional framework of the enlarged Union, the Nice European Council, in December 2000, called a new Intergovernmental Conference (IGC) to propose a new and extensive modification of the Treaties. In order to prepare the Intergovernmental Conference, the Laeken European Council (14-15 December 2001) decided to convene a **Convention on the Future of Europe**, with the former President of the French Republic, Mr Giscard d'Estaing as Chairman. The Convention brought together representatives of: the governments and national parliaments of the Member States and of all the institutions of the EC/EU. In order to widen the debate further and to involve all (interested) citizens, a Forum was made available to organisations representing civil society (the social partners, the business world, NGOs, academia, etc.).The Convention decided to call the treaty that it was preparing "**Treaty establishing a Constitution for Europe**". The results of the deliberations of the Convention were presented by its Chairman to the European Council meeting in Thessaloniki (19-20 June 2003), which welcomed the draft constitutional treaty and decided that it was a good basis for starting the work of the IGC.

The IGC, which began its work in Rome on October 2003 with the participation of representatives of twenty-five States, broadly took the proposals of the Convention on board and presented the draft of the Constitutional Treaty to the European Council, which adopted it with minor changes on 18 June 2004. The twenty-five heads of state or government of the enlarged Union **signed the new Treaty on 29 October 2004**, in Rome (venue chosen in commemoration of the original Treaty establishing the EEC). The new Treaty made provision to come into force two years after its signature, anticipating its ratification by the twenty-five Member States during this time. The negative referendums in France and the Netherlands, on 29 May and 1 June 2005, have certainly made this coming into force rather doubtful. However, we should know what it provides, because many of its good points might be used in a new treaty or Constitution in the future [see sections 7.2.3 and 7.2.4].

3.3.1. Why is the new Treaty called Constitutional?

For the first time in the history of European integration, the drafting of a treaty was entrusted to a Convention comprising a wide spectrum of the political forces of the Member States. Therefore, the first qualification of this Treaty as a constitutional one was the **extensive participation and the large consensus** of the political elite that characterised its elaboration. However, the citizens themselves were not involved in the deliberations on the drafting of the Constitutional Treaty, a failure that they rightly regret and would like to be corrected in the future [see section 7.2.4].

If it were to come into force, the Constitution **would simplify the European construction**. Once the new Treaty came into force, the existing Treaties on the European Union, the European Community and the European Atomic Energy Community would be repealed, thus eliminating the confusion between the Community and the Union. The Union would have a single legal personality under which it would negotiate, sign and implement all its external commitments, policies and activities, including trade, aid to development, representation in third countries and in international organisations and foreign and security policy. Both from the interior (its citizens) and from the exterior (its counterparts) the Union would, thus, be seen as a whole construction and not as a structure in pillars.

The Constitutional Treaty determines the **symbols which personify the Union**: the flag (a circle of twelve golden stars on a blue background); the anthem (based on the "Ode to Joy" from the Ninth Symphony by Ludwig van Beethoven); the motto ("United in diversity"); the currency (the euro); the Europe day (9 May). Although these emblems of European unification were adopted more or less informally in the past, their consecration in the Constitutional Treaty would symbolise the determination of the peoples of Europe "to transcend their former divisions and, united ever more closely, to forge a common destiny" (Preamble of the Constitution).

Other **important innovations** of this Treaty were the attribution of constitutional weight to the Charter for Fundamental Rights, the solemn acknowledgement of the Union's values and objectives, the definition of the conditions for membership of the Union (including conditions for voluntary withdrawal from the Union) and a clearer presentation of the principles determining the distribution of competences between the Union and its constituent parts [see section 3.3.2].

The Charter of the fundamental rights of European citizens as well as the provisions on participatory democracy and good governance would, through this Treaty, have acquired constitutional status, aiming at more democratic, transparent and controllable EU institutions that would be closer to the citizen. A Protocol on the application of the principles of subsidiarity and proportionality [see sections 5.1.2 and 5.1.3], which would have constitutional status, would provide for an "early-warning system" involving national parliaments in monitoring the legislative initiatives of the Commission [see sections 4.2.2 and 5.2.2]. Moreover, the Constitution would provide citizens with the right to invite the Commission to submit an appropriate proposal to the legislative authorities of the Union, if they could manage to collect one million signatures in a significant number of Member States.

3.3.2. How does the Constitution treat the question of the conferral of sovereign rights from the Member States to the Union?

The Constitutional Treaty does not depart from current practice on the question of transfer of sovereign rights from the Member States to the Union, but it **defines in detail the principles which govern this transfer** and guarantees that these principles should not be infringed. According to the Constitution, these principles are: the principle of conferral, under which the Union shall act within the limits of the competences conferred upon it by the Member States in the Constitution (Art. I-11) [see section 5.1.1]; the clear distinction of the Union's competences into areas of exclusive competence, of shared competence and of support of national policies (Art. I-13 to I-17); and the exercise of these competences in accordance with the principles of subsidiarity and proportionality under the control of national parliaments [see sections 5.1.2 and 5.1.3].

Under the **principle of conferral**, specified in the Constitutional Treaty, the Union shall act within the limits of the competences conferred upon it by the Member States in the Constitution, all other competences remaining with the Member States (Art. I-11). The flexibility of this principle is guaranteed by a clause allowing the Council, by unanimous vote and with the approval of the Parliament, to adopt measures necessary to attain any of the objectives laid down by the Constitution where there is no provision for powers of action to that effect in the Constitution (Art. I-18). This is to say that the Member States - and they alone - may confer to the Union parts of their sovereign powers, if and when they consider that their interests are better served by common action [see section 5.1.1].

The Constitution distinguishes between **three categories of Union competences**: exclusive, shared and supportive or coordinating. The areas of exclusive competence of the Union are: customs union and the common commercial policy, competition rules for the functioning of the internal market, monetary policy for the Member States whose currency is the euro and the conservation of marine biological resources (Art. I-13). In those areas, only the Union may legislate and the Member States may implement the Union acts. In the areas of shared competence, both the Union and the Member States may legislate, but the later may exercise their competence to the extent not covered by the Union competence (Art. I-14). The areas where the Union may take action in support or coordination of national policies are notably those of human health protection, industry, culture, tourism and education (Art. I-17). The competences of the Member States and of the Union in the area of the common foreign and security policy are specifically defined in the Constitution (Art. I-16).

Under the **principle of subsidiarity**, in areas which do not fall within its exclusive competence, the Union shall act only if and insofar as the objectives of the proposed action cannot be sufficiently achieved by the Member States, either at central level or at regional and local level, but can rather, by reason of the scale or effects of the proposed action, be better achieved at Union level. Under the **principle of proportionality**, the content and form of Union action shall not exceed that which is necessary to achieve the objectives of the Constitution (Art. I-11) [see sections 5.1.2 and 5.1.3].

The aforementioned principles were already guaranteed by the previous Treaties. However, the Constitutional Treaty introduces a major innovation in this regard, requiring that the **national parliaments be directly involved** in monitoring the proper application of the subsidiarity principle. The Protocol on the application of the principles of subsidiarity and proportionality, annexed to the Constitution, stipulates that the Commission must simultaneously send all its draft legislative acts and its amended drafts to the Union legislator and to the national parliaments. The reasons for concluding that a Union objective can be better achieved at Union level must be substantiated by qualitative and, wherever possible, quantitative indicators. If one third of the parliaments (or only a quarter if the proposal concerns the area of freedom, security and justice) feel that the draft European legislation does not comply with the principle of subsidiarity, the Commission or the institution from which the draft legislative act originates must review its proposal.

3.3.3. How does the Constitutional Treaty deal with common policies?

The European Union is not a federation of dependent states. It is a union of independent states and nations. It does not have federal institutions but common institutions. European integration is based on parts of national sovereignty that the Member States have agreed over time **to transfer to the shared sovereignty** of the Union. [see section 5.1.4]. The Constitution does not change these principles and, therefore, it does not make major changes to the existing common policies, which it calls "Union's policies" instead of "Community policies", as they are usually called now [see section 1.3.1]. However, the Constitution identifies clearly those areas where common policies predominate over national policies, those where common and national policies coexist and those where common policies support national policies.

In the **areas of exclusive competence**, the common policies of the Union prevail and Member States may only implement them and legislate solely if empowered by the Union. In the areas where the Union has a **competence shared with the Member States**, common policies exist side by side with national policies, but the Member States may legislate and act to the extent that the Union has not exercised its competence (Art. I-12). Consequently, in the areas of shared competence, the common policies frame and delimit the national policies. In certain areas the common policies of the Union may **support, coordinate or supplement the policies** of the Member States, without thereby superseding their competence in these areas (Art. I-17). In these areas, the coordination of national policies by common policies depends on the willingness of the Member States to confer new competences to the Union.

3.3.4. Which are the main institutional changes brought about by the Constitutional Treaty?

The Constitutional Treaty **strengthens the role of the European Parliament** in several ways [see section 4.3.2]. It jointly vests the Parliament and the Council of Ministers with the legislative and budgetary functions [see section 5.2.4]. Hence, if the Constitution would come into force, the Parliament would become co-legislator in almost all cases (95% of the legislative areas), with the exception of a dozen areas, where it would only be consulted. The request for accession of new Member States would be subject to the approval of the European Parliament, which could thus turn down a candidate, regardless of the unanimous approval of the governments of the Member States. According to the Constitution, the President of the Commission should be elected (not simply approved as happens now) by the majority of the members of the European Parliament, acting on a proposal from the European Council. This amendment would clearly establish the responsibility of the President of the Commission vis-à-vis the Parliament.

The Constitutional Treaty establishes a **permanent President of the European Council** [see section 4.1], who should be elected by qualified majority, for a term of two and a half years, renewable once, and should be responsible at his or her level for ensuring the external representation of the Union on issues concerning its common foreign and security policy. This Treaty also reorganises the **configurations of the Council of Ministers** [see section 4.4.1], separating the responsibilities of the Ministers of Foreign Affairs, who would deal with the external activities of the Union, from those of the Ministers of European affairs, who would ensure consistency in the work of the different Council configurations.

A main institutional innovation is the creation of the post of a **Union Minister for Foreign Affairs**, who would chair the Council of Ministers of Foreign Affairs, while being a Vice-President of the Commission and responsible within the Commission for external relations and for coordinating all aspects of the Union's external action. This function could considerably strengthen the Union's role in world affairs, in all areas (foreign policy, security and defence policies, commercial and aid to development policies) [see sections 6.4.5 and 6.4.6].

The Constitutional Treaty renames and **simplifies the legal instruments** of the Union. After its coming into force, the institutions would adopt European laws, European framework laws, European regulations, European decisions, recommendations and opinions (Art. I-33) [see section 5.3.3]. The **ordinary legislative procedure** extends very substantially the scope of the co-decision procedure [see section 5.2.4], thus giving the Parliament equal legislative powers with the Council of Ministers in practically all areas of the Union's activities, including the adoption of the budget, but excluding the common foreign and security policy.

3.3.5. Which are the main shortcomings of the Constitutional Treaty?

The Constitutional Treaty **could only mark some steps forward** in the long and slow process of European integration. It was elaborated at a certain point of time and in certain European and international circumstances to solve the problems arising from an ever growing membership and to allow the participating members to better defend their interests in these circumstances. However, the interests of the Member States are both objectively and subjectively quite different. In the Convention and in the Intergovernmental Conference, which adopted the draft Constitution, opinions differed widely between those who aspired for "more Europe" and those who wanted "less Europe". Compromise solutions had to be found to satisfy the minimal requirements of all sides. By definition, compromise solutions cannot be considered as ideal by any part in a negotiation. In these circumstances, the advantages of the Constitution, mentioned above, outweigh its shortcomings mentioned below.

The constitutional arrangements concerning **the external representation of the Union** are ambiguous. Article I-26 declares that the Commission ensures the Union's external representation [see section 4.2.4]. However, Article I-23, states that the President of the European Council shall ensure the external representation of the Union on issues concerning its common foreign and security policy, without prejudice to the powers of the Union Minister for Foreign Affairs, who according to Articles I-28 and I-40 shall conduct and put into effect the Union's common foreign and security policy [see section 6.4.6]. He or she shall conduct political dialogue with third parties on the Union's behalf and shall express the Union's position in international organisations and at international conferences. Who then of the two, the President of the European Council or the Minister for Foreign Affairs would actually represent the Union? The probable answer is that they would try to do it in tandem. This two-headed representation could work in most cases. But which of the two would prevail if the European Council - represented by its President - and the Commission - represented by its Vice-president and Minister for Foreign Affairs - who would be responsible before the European Parliament, had a different opinion about the interests of the Union in a matter of foreign policy?

The other problem concerning the **common foreign and security policy would be the rule of unanimity** in its decision-making, provided for in the Constitutional Treaty [see section 6.4.8]. The normal legislative instruments, European laws and framework laws are excluded and the Court of Justice has no competence, except in minor matters of CFSP. Hence, any Member State would have the right of veto and would not be bound to follow in its national policy the decisions agreed in common. These arrangements categorise the CFSP as an intergovernmental cooperation rather than as a common policy as its name seems to imply [see section 1.2.1]. There is therefore a contradiction between the aims of the CFSP as stated in the Constitution and the means that this Constitution gives this policy to pursue its objectives.

The Constitutional Treaty has, of course, many other shortcomings, such as the non direct election by the citizens of European

Commission members [see section 7.2.5] or the lack of a common policy for the information of the citizens concerning European affairs [see section 7.1.3]. These imperfections could, however be considered as minor and temporary, **if the Constitution could be easily amended in the future** to cope with problems that would arise in its implementation. The basic problem is that both the implementation and the amendment of this Constitution require the agreement of all the participants.

The Constitutional Treaty provides, indeed, that it must be **ratified by all the High Contracting Parties** in accordance with their respective constitutional requirements (Art. IV-447), which means that even if only one of them does not ratify it, this Treaty cannot enter into force. Its authors either were overoptimistic about the willingness of all Member States to ratify it or have knowingly handed it over bound in fetters to the will of even the most europhobic nation. These fetters might not be unbreakable, if this Treaty, like all Treaties and even all Constitutions, required the agreement of the representatives of the Member States, i.e. the national parliaments, and of them alone. However, the knots become Gordian, when some Member States ask by referendums the opinion of their peoples. A referendum may be a democratic way of agreement on a public policy, if the citizens know all the pros and the cons of that policy. But, if the citizens have no idea about the existing situation and about what the new Treaty is going to change, a referendum becomes a parody of popular will [see section 7.1.7].

It should be stressed that the requirement of unanimous ratification is an exception to normal practice for the ratification of both constitutions and treaties. A national constitution is normally adopted by a special majority, not the totality of the citizens or their representatives. Treaties are put into force after ratification by a certain number of the participating states, not by all of them. The exception to normal practices is a carry-over from the earlier times when a very few countries had to agree on the ways of conducting an experiment concerning a limited customs union [see section 2.1]. Since the experiment has become a successful enterprise, since it has expanded into new fields and has attracted a great number of participants [see section 2.2.2], **it is absurd to expect all of them to agree** on the ways to improve and develop the common enterprise [see section 7.1.7]. A company whose management would be thwarted by its rigid statutes would soon be outdistanced by its innovating and unrestrained competitors. Likewise, a union of nations competing in the world arena would be handicapped by its rigid statutes and its performances would never match those of its freer rivals. This then is the **major flaw of the project of the constitutional treaty**, a flaw that may render it stillborn, if one or a few Member States do not ratify it. If, on the other hand, it were ratified without any changes, it could block the further development of the process of European unification, since it would require the unanimity of twenty-five and soon more nations for its amendment.

Chapter 4

EUROPEAN GOVERNANCE

Common policies, which are the essence of the multinational integration process, are the fruit of intensive negotiations among the parties (member states), which participate in this process. In order to be acceptable to all parties, the conception of a common policy must try to satisfy or, at least, not harm the national interests of the parties and, therefore, **the governments of all member states must participate in the decision-making process**. Their participation, however, may be direct or indirect. Decisions on fundamental common policies, requiring new transfers of national sovereignties to the shared or supranational sovereignty [see section 1.3.2], are taken by the participating governments (in intergovernmental conferences) and are outlined in treaties, signed by those governments and ratified by them after authorisation by the national parliaments.

Decisions on secondary common policies, i.e. those needed to attain the goals set in the treaty, including policy guidelines and legal acts based on the treaty, are taken by the **common institutions** set up by the treaty, according to procedures and following the legal forms agreed in this treaty [see section 5.3.1]. In contrast to an organisation based on intergovernmental cooperation, where the governments are the main actors [see section 1.2.1], in a multinational integration process the governments of the member states direct the play from the backstage, but they leave the stage to the actors, that is their representatives in the common institutions, appointed by them and/or by their citizens.

The principal actors of European integration are **called "institutions" by the European Treaties**. However, the qualification of an organ as institutional is changing in various revisions of the Treaties following the development of the European Community/Union [see chapter 3]. According to the EC Treaty (Nice version) the basic institutional structure of the European Union consists of five institutions: the European Parliament, the Council of Ministers, the Commission, the Court of Justice and the Court of

Auditors. According to the Constitutional Treaty the institutional framework comprises: the European Parliament, the European Council, the Council of Ministers, the European Commission and the Court of Justice of the European Union. The European Council is therefore recognised by the Constitution as a fully-fledged institution, but the Court of Auditors is not included in the basic institutional framework. It is included in the "other institutions and advisory bodies", as is the European Central Bank (ECB). The constitutional Treaty (like the EC Treaty) recognises the status of "advisory bodies" to the Economic and Social Committee and to the Committee of the Regions.

For analytical purposes, we consider as **principal actors of European integration** the five organs which intervene principally in the decision-making process and therefore in the governance of the Community/Union: the European Council, which sets the goals of the common policies; the European Commission, which makes the proposals for the decisions to be taken and is mainly responsible for the implementation of the common policies; the European Parliament and the Council of Ministers, which take the decisions; and the Court of Justice, which controls the legality of these decisions.

4.1. The European Council

4.1.1. What is the composition of the European Council?

The European Council consists of the **Heads of State** (the President of the French Republic and the Presidents of the Republics of Cyprus, Latvia and Lithuania, responsible for foreign and European affairs) **or of Government** (the Prime Ministers of the other Member States) of the EU and the President of the European Commission. Begun on an informal basis as "Summit meetings" in the early 1960s, the European Council is now explicitly provided for in Article 4 of the Treaty on European Union (Nice). This Article provides that the European Council shall meet at least twice a year, under the chairmanship of the Head of State or Government of the Member State which holds the Presidency of the Council. Departing from the letter of the Treaty, the European Council agreed in June 2002 that it shall meet in principle four times a year (twice every six months) and that, in exceptional circumstances, it may hold an extraordinary meeting. European Council meetings are prepared by the General Affairs and External Relations Council [see section 4.4.1], which coordinates all the preparatory work and draws up the agenda. The Presidency ensures that meetings proceed smoothly. At those meetings the Heads of State or Government and the President of the Commission are assisted by the Ministers of Foreign Affairs and one Member of the Commission.

Apart from considering the European Council as a main institution of the Union, **the Constitutional Treaty provided for a permanent President** of the European Council, who would take on the work currently assigned to rotating Presidencies [see section 3.3.4]. He or she would be elected by qualified majority, for a term of two and a half years, renewable once (Art. I-22). This new institutional arrangement was designed to lend a degree of visibility and stability to the Presidency of the European Council. The Permanent President would necessarily have the same nationality as one of the members of the European Council, but would not participate in the voting procedure within this institution. Since he or she would not hold a national office, the President would have the freedom of time and spirit to conduct the necessary discussions and negotiations with the twenty-five (and soon more) heads of government, usually in their respective capitals, before the meetings of the European Council. Thus, according to the Constitution, the President should be able to facilitate cohesion and consensus and drive forward the work of the European Council.

4.1.2. What are the functions of the European Council?

The European Council is the architect of European construction. It provides the Union with the necessary impetus for its development; it defines the general political guidelines thereof and resolves the most important problems of the construction. The European Council is above all **a forum for free and informal exchanges of views** between the responsible leaders of the Member States. Its strength is its spontaneity and its informality, which bring about a sort of "esprit de corps" on the part of Europe's political leaders. Being a venue where package deals can be struck, and thus being free from the stiffness that sometimes paralyses the proceedings of the Council of Ministers, the European Council often acts as an appeal body for politically and economically important business which is deadlocked at ministerial level.

It should be noted, however, that the Heads of State or Government **do not adopt legal acts formally binding** the Member States. Their deliberations result in the publication of declarations containing guidelines and general directives for future Community action. These declarations have undeniable political value, but no legal binding force. They give the political impetus necessary for common policies, but the latter are constructed with Community provisions adopted subsequently in accordance with the procedures laid down in the EC and Euratom Treaties [see section 5.2.1]. The situation is quite different in the sphere of the common foreign and security policy where the European Council, in addition to adopting common strategies, can decide upon joint actions or common positions, which bind politically, but not legally, the Member States [see section 6.4.6].

The Constitution does not change much the functions of the European Council. Normally, the latter will not exercise legislative functions. All European laws or framework laws must be adopted by the Council of Ministers, in most cases jointly with the European Parliament. However, the European Council can also be called upon to debate a legislative act in cases which are clearly defined in the Constitution (so-called "emergency brake" procedure). In addition, the Constitution stipulates that certain decisions, of a more constitutional nature, will be taken by the European Council, such as those relating to the composition of the European Parliament (Article I-20), the arrangements for the rotating Presidency of the Council (Article I-24), and the suspension of the rights of a Member State in the event of a serious and persistent breach of the values of the Union (Article I-59). The President of the European Council will ensure the external representation of the Union on issues concerning common foreign and security policy, without prejudice to the responsibilities of the Minister for Foreign Affairs.

4.2. The European Commission

4.2.1. What is the composition of the European Commission?

From the very beginning of the Community until 2004, the European Commission, **usually referred to simply as the Commission**, was made up of two nationals from each "big" and one national from each "small" Member State. Hence, the Treaty of Nice - adopted at a time when the European Community/Union numbered fifteen Member States [see section 3.2.3], five of which were considered as big (Germany, France, the UK, Italy and Spain) - stated that "the Commission shall consist of 20 Members, who shall be chosen on the grounds of their general competence and whose independence is beyond doubt" (Article 213 TEC). Anticipating the enlargement of the EC/EU, this Treaty provided, however, that the number of members of the Commission could be altered by the Council, acting unanimously. In fact, in the Act of Accession of the ten new Member States (article 45), it was agreed (not without difficulties) that any State acceding to the Union should be entitled to have one of its nationals as a member of the Commission and that a new Commission composed of one national of each Member State should take up its duties on 1 November 2004, after the European elections of June 2004.

Thus, **actually, the Commission is composed of 25 members** (Commissioners), who are proposed by the government of each Member State and are appointed, for a period of five years, by common accord of all the governments and may not, during their term of office, engage in any other occupation, whether gainful or not. They must not take instructions from any government and all governments must respect this principle and not seek to influence the members of the Commission in the performance of their tasks (Art. 213 TEC) [see section 5.2.2].

The Heads of State or Government, acting by a qualified majority, nominate the President of the Commission and the nomination must be approved by the European Parliament. The President and the other Members of the Commission are subject as a body to a **vote of approval by the European Parliament** (Art. 214 TEC). The Parliament appraises every Commissioner as to his or her programme and ideas and may put forward objections as to his/her suitability for his/her particular responsibilities inside the Commission, but may not reject his/her appointment. Hence, in case of objections expressed by the Parliament for certain members of the Commission, its President has the option of either assigning other responsibilities to the members in question or of risking the rejection of the whole body by the Parliament.

The Constitutional Treaty provides that the current composition of the Commission – one Commissioner per Member State – is maintained until 2014. From then on, if this Treaty is put into force, the Commission shall consist of a number of members, including its President and the Union Minister for Foreign Affairs [see section 6.4.8], corresponding to two thirds of the number of Member States, unless the European Council, acting unanimously, decides to alter this number. The members of the Commission shall be selected from among the nationals of the Member States on the basis of a system of equal rotation between the Member States, guaranteeing equal treatment and reflecting the demographic and geographical range of all the Member States (art. I-26).

According to the Constitution, **the President of the Commission shall be proposed to the European Parliament** by the European Council, acting by a qualified majority [see section 5.2.6]. The Parliament may elect the candidate, acting by a majority of its component members. If he or she does not obtain the required majority, the European Council, acting by a qualified majority, shall within one month propose a new candidate who shall be elected by the European Parliament following the same procedure (art. I-27). The President, the Union Minister for Foreign Affairs and the other members of the Commission shall be subject as a body to a vote of consent by the European Parliament (art. I-27).

4.2.2. What is the role of the Commission in the decision-making process?

The Commission is the driving force for European integration. Under the Community decision-making process provided for in the European Community Treaty, it alone **has the initiative to make proposals** with a view to the taking of Community decisions [see section 5.2.2]. No other body and no individual State can replace the Commission in this task. It alone can amend its proposal, with the sole exception of there being unanimity in the Council to do so. On the basis of the political impetus given by the European Council with declarations and often by the European Parliament with resolutions, it is the task of the Commission to make proposals to the

Council and to the Parliament to undertake new activities in the framework of the Treaties. The **power of initiative**, which is held by the Commission, is particularly important for the development of the common policies and therefore for the progress of the multinational integration process. All common policies, all Community legislation, all Community programmes have been adopted by the legislative bodies with Commission initiatives.

In its proposals, the Commission is entrusted with the **task of defining the common interest** in each policy, legal measure or action that it proposes and the representatives of the Member States can only unanimously substitute it in this role [see section 5.2.3]. This means that even if only one state believes that the amendment to the proposal of the Commission, promoted by the majority of the Member States, is contrary to its interests, the proposal cannot be adopted by the Council with qualified majority voting. The proposal must be amended by the Commission itself, which must find a compromise solution that comes closer to the common interest. Of course, if the Commission considers that the minority is exaggerating or filibustering, it can amend its proposal in the sense wanted by the majority, which may thus adopt it. In most cases, however, in the course of the deliberations and negotiations within the Council, the Commission amends its proposal repeatedly in order to encourage concessions here and there and thus reach agreement.

It should be stressed, however, that all legal acts and decisions of the European Community are taken, usually in tandem, by the European Parliament and the Council with the codecision procedure or, in some cases, by the Council alone, i.e. by the representatives of the Member States. **The Commission does not legislate**. On the one hand, it proposes legal or administrative measures. On the other hand, it implements the acts and decisions taken by the Member States themselves through their representatives in the Parliament and the Council [see section 5.2.4]. The slogan concerning "the laws taken by the technocrats of Brussels" is a myth well cultivated by europhobic media. The fault of the Commission and the Member States is that they have not adopted a common policy for the information and education of the citizens, in order to fight this and other myths propagated by the enemies of European unification [see section 7.1.6].

The Constitution confirms the near monopoly of the legislative initiative of the Commission. It specifies that the Commission shall promote the general interest of the Union and take appropriate initiatives to that end. Union legislative acts shall be adopted only on the basis of a Commission proposal, except where the Constitution provides otherwise [see section 5.3.3]. Other acts shall be adopted on the basis of a Commission proposal where the Constitution so provides (Art. I-26). It can be inferred that the governments of the Member States, which have signed the Constitutional Treaty, have appreciated the work of the Commission to date and agreed to place it as the arbitrator and conciliator of their national interests.

4.2.3. What are the other functions of the European Commission?

The Commission is the **guardian of the Treaties** and of the "acquis communautaire" (i.e., all the Community's legislation). One of its main tasks is to ensure fulfilment of the obligations of the Member States and/or proper application by them of the provisions of the Treaties and of secondary legislation (Art 226 TEC). For that purpose it has investigative power, which it exercises at its own initiative or in response to a request from a government or a complaint from an individual. If, following its investigation, the Commission considers that there is **infringement of Community legislation**, it invites the State concerned to give explanations and, if these are not satisfactory, it refers the matter to the Court of Justice [see section 4.5.3], which arbitrates the dispute and, more often than not, sanctions the irregularity as noted by the Commission. There are often differences of opinion between the Member States and the Commission, but the Commission's impartiality in respect of the various Member States has never been called into question [see section 5.2.3].

The Commission is also the **executive body** of the Community and plays, therefore, an **administrative role**. The Treaties confer upon the Commission extensive powers of execution to ensure the attainment of the objectives set out in them: good functioning of the single market, control of the rules of competition, supply of fissile materials, etc. But the Commission's powers are constantly increased by the powers conferred to it by the Council for the implementation of common policies (Art. 202 TEC). It is the Commission which implements the decisions of the legislative bodies (the Parliament and the Council) [see section 5.2.4]. These implementation decisions of the Commission usually take the form of the main decisions (regulation, directive or decision) [see section 5.3.1]. The Commission proposes to the legislative bodies and manages the Community budget and in particular the various Community Funds [see section 5.4.4].

The Constitutional Treaty confirms all the above tasks of the Commission. It asserts that this institution shall ensure the application of the Constitution, and measures adopted by the institutions pursuant to the Constitution (Art I-26). On these subjects, again, the governments of the Member States demonstrate their satisfaction with the functioning of the Commission to date, since they declare in the Constitution, which they have signed, that they wish to continue to get the services that it provides.

4.2.4. What is the role of the Commission in external policies?

The Commission plays a **representative role** by ensuring the representation of the European Union in third countries and in many international organisations. The role of the Commission is particularly important in the conduct of the common commercial policy and of the aid to development policy. Acting on behalf of the Community on instructions from the Council, the Commission negotiates tariff agreements, in the context of the World Trade Organisation (WTO), trade agreements with third countries, association and partnership agreements and the agreements on the accession of new member states to the European Union. In order to carry out its representative role, the Commission has its own representations in more than 160 countries with which the EC/EU has diplomatic relations and in several international organisations.

The **Constitutional Treaty** affirms that, with the exception of the common foreign and security policy (CFSP) [see section 6.4.5], and other cases provided for in the Constitution, the Commission shall ensure the Union's external representation (Art. I-26). But, the exclusion of the CFSP from the external tasks of the Commission is relative, since the **Union Minister for Foreign Affairs** will have the power of proposal and will, thus, have a strong voice in the development of the Union's common foreign and security policy, which should be conducted and carried out as mandated by the Council [see section 6.4.6]. The same will apply to the common security and defence policy (Art I-28) [see section 6.4.7]. Indeed, the Union Minister for Foreign Affairs will play a dual role, one in the Commission, as its Vice-President, and one in the Foreign Affairs Council, as its President [see section 6.4.8]. He or she shall be responsible within the Commission for tasks incumbent on it in external relations and for coordinating other aspects of the Union's external action. Within the Council, he or she shall ensure the consistency of the Union's external action.

4.3. The European Parliament

4.3.1. What is the composition of the European Parliament?

During the early years of European construction, the Members of the European Parliament (MEPs) were appointed by the national parliaments and had to be members of them. Although it was provided for by the Treaties of Paris and Rome, election of the European Parliament by **direct universal suffrage** only became a reality in June 1979. Henceforth, European elections are held in June every five years. Common electoral principles, applicable from 2004, provide for elections to be held by direct universal suffrage, freely and in secret, and for Members of the European Parliament to be elected on the basis of proportional representation using the list system or the single transferable vote, their office being incompatible with that of member of a national parliament.

The number of Members of the European Parliament has increased with the successive enlargements of the Community/Union. After the 2004 enlargement, **the number of seats was increased to 732. They are allocated as follows:**

- 99 to Germany;
- 78 each to France, Italy and the United Kingdom;
- 54 each to Spain and Poland;
- 27 to the Netherlands;
- 24 each to Belgium, the Czech Republic, Greece, Hungary and Portugal;
- 19 to Sweden;
- 18 to Austria;
- 14 each to Denmark, Slovakia and Finland;
- 13 each to Ireland and Lithuania;
- 9 to Latvia;
- 7 to Slovenia;
- 6 each to Cyprus, Estonia and Luxembourg; and
- 5 to Malta.

The Constitution lays down that the maximum number of seats of the European Parliament should be 750, even after new accessions. It does not lay down the detailed breakdown of seats between the Member States. Instead, it establishes an allocation rule which states that **representation of citizens is degressively proportional** (Article I-20). No Member State shall be allocated more than 96 seats, while the minimum number of seats per Member State is to be 6, in order to make sure that, even in the least populous Member States, all the major shades of political opinion will have a chance of being represented in the European Parliament. This rule implies that to make room for the representatives of new Member States, the more populous actual members will have to give up a number of seats. A European decision, based on a proposal of the Parliament itself, will implement this rule. This means, on the one hand, that the Parliament will control its own composition and, on the other, that in the case of future enlargements, the Constitution will not need to be modified in order to specify the distribution of seats in the Parliament.

4.3.2. What are the functions of the European Parliament?

Thanks to its direct election by the peoples of the Union, the European Parliament is the only really multinational legislative assembly in the world and plays an increasingly important role in the European integration process. In fact, although under the original Treaties the Parliament's role was purely advisory [see section 3.1], it has kept growing by virtue of the increasing political influence it has gradually managed to secure. At present **it exercises four functions**: legislative, political, supervisory and budgetary.

The European Parliament's first task under the Treaties establishing the original Communities, that of **consultation**, whereby Parliament gives its opinion on Commission proposals, was strengthened by the European Single Act of 1987 [see section 3.1.2], which introduced a procedure of cooperation with the Council in many Community decisions. The **legislative function** of the Parliament was considerably increased with the Treaties of Amsterdam and Nice. Article 192 (TEC) provides, in fact, for the participation of the European Parliament in the process leading up to the adoption of Community acts through exercise of its powers under the procedures laid down in Articles 251 and 252 (co-decision and cooperation) [see section 5.2.4]. Furthermore, the Parliament has the right to give or withhold its **assent** as regards the conclusion of certain international agreements and the accession of new Member States, thus participating in the definition of the Community's foreign policy.

The **political function** of the Parliament is also essential. As it represents 450 million citizens (EU-25) and is the foremost European forum, the Parliament is the virtual contractor for European construction. It often calls upon the other protagonists, the Commission and the Council, to develop or alter existing common policies or to initiate new ones. Indeed, the Treaty gives it the right to request that the Commission submit any appropriate proposals on matters on which it considers a Community act is required (Art. 192 TEC) [see section 4.2.2]. Should the Commission or the Council fail to act as required for the purpose of implementing the Treaty, the Parliament may initiate proceedings against them before the European Court of Justice [see section 4.5.3]. The Commission and the Council have to report to the Parliament for their acts. The European Council itself reports to the Parliament on each of its meetings and annually on the progress achieved by the Union.

The **monitoring function** of the Parliament is exercised in particular vis-à-vis the Commission. The President and the other members of the Commission are subject as a body to a vote of approval by the European Parliament (Art. 214 TEC). The Commission is answerable to the Parliament alone, so as to obviate its bowing before the will of the national governments or of some of them. The Commission has to account to the European Parliament, defend its position before parliamentary commissions and in plenary sessions. The Parliament may, at the request of a quarter of its Members, set up a temporary Committee of Inquiry to investigate alleged contraventions or maladministration in the implementation of Community law (Art. 193 TEC). In case of a serious maladministration, the Parliament may pass a motion of censure against the Commission by a two-thirds majority of its members and thus compel it to resign (Art 201 TEC). The European Parliament appoints an Ombudsman empowered to receive complaints from any citizen of the Union concerning instances of maladministration in the activities of the Community institutions or bodies (Art. 195 TEC).

As regards **budgetary functions**, the Parliament has to give its agreement to any major decision involving expenditure to be borne by the Community budget [see section 5.4]. It is effectively the Parliament which, at the end of a conciliation procedure with the Council, adopts or rejects the budget proposed by the Commission. Thus, it exercises a democratic control on the own resources of the Community [see section 5.4.2]. It also monitors Community expenditure, since it has the power to give a discharge to the Commission for the management of the Community budget (Art. 272 and 276 TEC).

The **Constitutional Treaty enhances significantly the functions of the European Parliament**. It extends the codecision procedure, renamed "ordinary legislative procedure", to a large number of articles [see section 5.2.4]. The Parliament would thus become co-legislator in almost all laws and framework laws of the Union, with the exception of a dozen cases, where it will only be consulted. The law determining the annual budget of the Union will be adopted jointly by the EP and the Council, with the Parliament having the final word on the budget as a whole (Article III-404). The European Parliament will thus have practically the same legislative and budgetary functions as a national parliament.

The Constitution also reinforces the functions of **political control of the Parliament vis-à-vis the Commission**. It lays down that the President of the Commission will be elected by the European Parliament by a majority of its members, acting on a proposal from the European Council, which should take into account the results of the European elections. The Parliament could turn down the candidate proposed by the European Council and force it to propose another personality for President of the Commission. The President, the Union Minister for Foreign Affairs [see section 6.4.8] and the other members of the Commission will be subject as a body to a vote of consent by the European Parliament (Art I-27), which means that the Parliament may reject the composition of the Commission arranged by its President and force him or her to review it. With a motion of censure, carried by a two-thirds majority of the votes cast, representing a majority of its component members, the European Parliament may force the members of the Commission to resign as a body (Art III-340). These procedures would make the responsibility of the Commission vis-à-vis the Parliament resemble that of a government vis-à-vis a national parliament.

Thus, if the Constitutional Treaty were ever to come into force, the functions of the European Parliament would resemble those of the national parliaments, which, even if they have more rights than it in constitutional terms, often exercise them less vigorously, due to the allegiance of the majority of their members to the governing party or parties.

4.4. The Council of Ministers

4.4.1. What is the composition of the Council?

The **Council** is composed of a representative of each Member State at ministerial level, authorised to commit the government of that Member State (Art 203 TEC). While it is usually referred to broadly as "the Council" or "the Council of Ministers", it actually consists of **nine specialised configurations** regrouping several related areas, e.g. general affairs and external relations or economic and financial affairs. Each Council configuration is composed of the ministers with responsibility in the matter, but several ministers may participate as full members of the same Council configuration, e.g. the ministers responsible for health and social policy.

Although Commission proposals are discussed inside the specialised Council configurations, decisions agreed by all the Member States can be taken without a debate (as "points A" in the agenda) by any Council whatsoever, and this is often the "**General Affairs and External Relations Council**", composed of the Ministers of Foreign Affairs. This is the principle Council configuration and holds separate meetings (with separate agendas and possibly on different dates) dealing, respectively, with: (a) preparation for and follow-up to the European Council meetings, institutional and administrative questions, horizontal dossiers which affect several of the Union's policies; and (b) the whole of the Union's external action, namely common foreign and security policy, foreign trade, development cooperation and humanitarian aid.

The **Council Presidency** changes every six months to another country in alphabetical order, and it is therefore the Minister of the country holding the Presidency who chairs each Council meeting. The rotation of the Presidency has the advantage of giving each country a chance to prove its efficiency in promoting common policies, on the basis of Commission proposals, thus encouraging emulation among the Member States in the advancement of European integration.

The Council is assisted by a General Secretariat, consisting of "Eurocrats" of all the nationalities of the Union, separate from their counterparts in the Commission but organised in a similar way. The Council is also assisted by many working parties of national civil servants, which examine the proposals of the Commission and report to the **Permanent Representatives Committee (COREPER).** This committee sits in two parts consisting of the Ambassadors of the Member States and their deputies and is responsible for preparing the work of the Council and for carrying out the tasks assigned to it by the Council (Art. 207 TEC).

The **Constitutional Treaty** confirms that the Council shall meet in different configurations and mentions specifically the two principal ones: the General Affairs Council and the Foreign Affairs Council (Art. I-24). This represents a subject-based splitting of the present General Affairs and External Relations Council. The General Affairs Council would be responsible for ensuring consistency in the work of the various Council configurations and the follow-up to meetings of the European Council. The Foreign Affairs Council, chaired by the Union's Minister for Foreign Affairs, would adopt the European decisions necessary for defining and implementing the common foreign and security policy (CFSP).

4.4.2. What are the functions of the Council?

On the basis of the original Treaties [see section 3.1], the Council was the only legislative authority of the Community and this was the main reason for the then existing democratic deficit of the Community [see section 5.2.5]. Subsequent amendments of the Treaties have joined, ever more closely, the European Parliament in the decision-making process, thus making the Council **one of the two legislative authorities** and reducing, consequently, the democratic deficit. Going a step further, the **Constitutional Treaty** specifies that the Council shall, jointly with the European Parliament, exercise legislative and budgetary functions (Art. I-23) [see section 5.2.4]. Hence, the legislative functions of the Council would come close to those of an Upper House or Senate, representing the governments of the Member States, and sharing these functions with the European Parliament, representing directly the peoples of the Union.

However, in addition to its legislative and budgetary functions, the Council ensures coordination of the general economic policies of the Member States and plays an important role in defining and implementing the common foreign and security policy (CFSP) [see section 6.4.6]. According to the Constitution, the Council and the Union Minister for Foreign Affairs should ensure that CFSP principles are complied with by the Member States (Art. III-294).

4.5. The Court of Justice

4.5.1. What is the composition of the Court of Justice?

The Court of Justice consists, in fact, of two bodies, with their seat in Luxembourg: the Court of Justice proper and the Court of First Instance. **The Court of Justice**, often called European Court of Justice (ECJ) consists of one judge per Member State. It sits in chambers or in a Grand Chamber, in accordance with the rules laid down in its Statutes. It is assisted by Advocates-General (Art. 221 TEC). The **Court of First Instance** comprises at least one judge per Member State. The number of Judges is determined by the Statute of the Court of Justice, which may provide for the Court of First Instance to be assisted by Advocates-General (Art. 224 TEC).

The Judges and Advocates-General of the Court of Justice and of the Court of First Instance are chosen from persons whose independence is beyond doubt and who possess the qualifications required for appointment to the highest judicial offices in their respective countries or who are jurisconsults of recognised competence. They are appointed by common accord of the governments of the Member States for a term of six years. Every three years there is a partial replacement of the Judges and Advocates-General (Art 223 TEC).

According to the **Constitutional Treaty**, the Court of Justice of the European Union shall include the Court of Justice, the General Court and specialised courts. Hence, the term "Court of Justice of the European Union" would officially designate the two levels of jurisdiction taken together. The supreme body would be called the "Court of Justice" while the Court of First Instance would be renamed "General Court" (Art. I-29). The Court of Justice shall consist of one judge from each Member State. It shall be assisted by Advocates-General. The General Court shall include at least one judge per Member State, which means that the number of its judges may be greater than the number of the Member States and thus it may include judges of the same nationality.

4.5.2. What is the role of the Court of Justice?

In a community of states the common rules adopted by the decision-making bodies might be interpreted and applied differently from country to country, if only national courts controlled them. Therefore, the general task assigned to the Court of Justice and to the Court of First Instance is to ensure that Community **law is observed in a uniform manner** in the interpretation and application of the Treaty, of the legal acts and of the decisions adopted by the Council and the Parliament or by the Commission (Art. 220 to 245 TEC).

The judgments of the Court of Justice reflect the **vitality of European law**. They reinforce the strength of this law and provide it with the necessary authority vis-à-vis governments, national judiciaries, parliaments and citizens. Although European law is a statute law passed by legislative bodies, it is often amended by them in accordance with the case law of the Court of Justice. The Court plays therefore an important role in the European integration process by clarifying ambiguous legal provisions, adopted sometimes under the pressure of reaching agreement between law-makers of different cultures defending various interests.

4.5.3. What are the tasks of the Court of Justice?

The **Court of First Instance (CFI)** has jurisdiction in all actions brought by natural or legal persons and cases relating notably to agriculture, fisheries, the European Funds (regional, social), transport and State aids. The judgments of the CFI can form the subject of appeals, confined to points of law, to the Court of Justice (Art. 225 TEC).

Being the supreme court of the Communities, the **Court of Justice** not only gives a coherent and uniform interpretation of European law, but it ensures that all the Member States and their citizens comply with it. Apart from the tendency of governments to interpret European law in the interest of their nations, it is new law and not always well known. The national judges, who are the judges of first instance of the rules and behaviour relative to European law, may turn to the Court of Justice by means of a **referral for a preliminary ruling** to ask it to adopt a position on the interpretation or evaluation of the validity of the provisions of European acts. Through its preliminary rulings, the Court plays the role of a legal council whose opinions are binding on the parties concerned.

Disputes falling within the unlimited jurisdiction of the Court are made up in particular of cases relating to non-compliance or to the interpretation of the Community's rules of competition. In the legal field itself the Court reviews the legality of Community acts. **Proceedings for annulment** may be brought against the decision-making institutions (Council or Council/Parliament and Commission) either by a Member State, or by another institution or even, in certain instances, by an individual. **Proceedings for failure to act**, on the other hand, are aimed at securing a ruling where the Council or the Commission has failed to meet its obligation to act, thus infringing the provisions of the Treaties. **Proceedings for infringement** of Community law may be brought by Community institutions (in practice, the Commission), a Member State or an individual.

The **Constitutional Treaty** confirms the present tasks of the "Court of Justice" and of the Court of First Instance, renamed "General Court" (Art. I-29). However, the Constitution stipulates that any natural or legal person may institute proceedings against "a regulatory act which is of direct concern to him or her and does not entail implementing measures" (Article III-365), thus making it easier for citizens to challenge the Union's regulatory acts under which penalties are imposed, even if these acts do not affect them individually.

4.6. Other institutions and bodies

The institutions of the EC/EU are evolving along with the evolution of European integration. Of the institutions and advisory bodies that we consider in this section, only the European Economic and Social Committee was provided in the original Treaties [see section 3.1.]. New institutions and bodies have been created to cover new needs, notably the Committee of the Regions and the European Central Bank. The Court of Auditors is considered as a main institution by the Treaty of Nice, but not by the Constitutional Treaty, probably because it does not participate in the decision-making process.

4.6.1. What is the structure and what are the functions of the European Central Bank?

In the framework of the economic and monetary union that it has launched, the Treaty of Maastricht [see section 3.2.1] has established a **European system of central banks (ESCB)** and a **Euro-**

pean Central Bank (ECB). The two organs are closely associated. They act within the limits of the powers conferred upon them by the EC Treaty and by the Statute of the ESCB and of the ECB annexed thereto (Art. 8 TEC). The ESCB is composed of the ECB and of the national central banks and is governed by the decision-making bodies of the ECB which are the Governing Council and the Executive Board (Art 107 TEC). The Governing Council is composed of the Governors of the central banks of all the Member States of the EC/EU, whereas the President, the Vice-President and the other members of the Executive Board of the ECB are appointed by common accord of the governments of the Member States, which have adopted the euro. Neither the ECB, nor a national central bank may seek or take instructions from Community institutions or bodies, from any government of a Member State or from any other body (Art. 108 TEC).

The objectives of the ESCB are, primarily, to maintain price stability and, without prejudice to this objective, to support the general economic policies in the Community (Art. 105 TEC). The basic tasks of the ESCB are: to define and implement the monetary policy of the Community, to conduct foreign-exchange operations, to hold and manage the official foreign reserves of the Member States and to promote the smooth operation of payment systems. The ECB, which has legal personality, has the exclusive right to authorise the issue of banknotes within the Community's eurozone (Art. 106 TEC). In order to carry out the tasks entrusted to the ESCB, the ECB may: make regulations to the extent necessary to implement the tasks defined in the Treaty, take decisions necessary for carrying out the tasks entrusted to the ESCB and make recommendations and deliver opinions (Art 110 TEC).

The **Constitution** gives the European Central Bank the status of an institution, in order to emphasise its independence. It brings together the general provisions on the ECB and the ESCB, without introducing any substantive changes. Accepting the fact that not all the EU Member States need to adopt the euro as their currency [see section 6.3.3], the Constitution declares that the European Central Bank, together with the national central banks of the Member States whose currency is the euro, which constitute the Eurosystem, shall conduct the monetary policy of the Union, while those Member States whose currency is not the euro, and their central banks, shall retain their powers in monetary matters (Art I-30).

4.6.2. What is the structure and what are the functions of the Court of Auditors?

The Court of Auditors consists of one national from each Member State, chosen from among persons who belong or have belonged in their respective countries to external audit bodies or who are especially qualified for this office. Their independence must be beyond doubt (Art 247 TEC).

The Court of Auditors **examines the accounts of all revenue and expenditure of the Community**, particularly the annual budget managed by the Commission, and of all bodies set up by the Community [see section 5.4]. It examines in particular whether all revenue has been received and all expenditure incurred in a lawful and regular manner and must report on any cases of irregularity. The Court of Auditors **draws up an annual report** after the close of each financial year. This is forwarded to the other institutions of the Community and is published, together with the replies of these institutions to the observations of the Court of Auditors, in the Official Journal of the European Union. The annual and the specific reports of the Court of Auditors are acknowledged to be a valuable input to Parliament's debates on the discharge to be given to the Commission for its execution of the budget [see section 5.4.4].

The **Constitutional Treaty** does not modify the structure and the functions of the Court of Auditors. It confirms its status as an independent institution, which shall examine the accounts of all Union revenue and expenditure, and shall ensure good financial management (Articles I-31, III-384 and III-385). The only significant change is that it requires the Court to send its annual report to national parliaments, for information, thus increasing the democratic control of the Union's finances.

4.6.3. What is the structure and what are the functions of the Economic and Social Committee?

The Economic and Social Committee (ESC) is made up of 317 members proposed by the governments of the Member States. Germany, France, Italy and the United Kingdom propose 24 members each; Spain and Poland 21; Belgium, the Czech Republic, Greece, Hungary, Netherlands, Portugal, Austria and Sweden 12 each; Denmark, Ireland, Lithuania, Slovakia and Finland 9 each; Estonia, Latvia and Slovenia 7 each; Cyprus and Luxembourg 6 each; and Malta 5.

The members of the ESC are appointed by the Council after consulting the Commission. They must provide a **wide representation of the various categories of economic and social life** (Art. 257-262 TEC) and divide voluntarily into three groups: the Employers' Group (known as "Group I"), which is made up of representatives of industry, banking or financial institutions, transport operators' federations, etc.; the Workers' Group (known as "Group II"), mainly composed of representatives of trade union organisations; and the Various Interests Group (known as "Group III"), which comprises representatives of agriculture, skilled trades, small and medium-sized enterprises, the professions, consumer associations and organisations representing various interests, such as families or ecological movements. However, the members of the Committee are not elected by the corresponding national groups but are appointed by the governments. This is a flaw that should be corrected in the interest of the democratic legitimacy of the ESC.

The Committee is the official body which enables the Community institutions to evaluate and take into account in the conception of common policies the **interests of the various economic and social groups**. The Committee must be consulted by the Council or by the Commission in certain areas provided for by the Treaty establishing the European Community. The Committee may be consulted by these institutions in all cases where they consider it appropriate. Furthermore, the ESC may issue an opinion at its own initiative when it considers such action appropriate (Art. 262 TEC). Whether they are requested by the Commission or the Council or issued at its own initiative, the Committee's opinions are not binding on the institutions, a shortcoming that weakens their significance. However, the Committee plays the role of a forum in which the interests of the various socio-professional categories, rather than national interests, are expressed officially and assessed.

The **Constitutional Treaty** does not make any fundamental changes to the structure and functions of the Economic and Social Committee, other than lengthening the term of office of its members to five years, so as to coincide with that of the members of the European Parliament. It limits the number of members of the Committee to 350, notwithstanding future enlargements, and specifies that the composition of the Committee will be determined by a European decision adopted unanimously by the Council on a proposal from the Commission (Art. III-389). Before adopting the list of members drawn up in accordance with the proposals made by each Member State, the Council may obtain the opinion of European bodies which are representative of the various economic and social sectors and of civil society to which the Union's activities are of concern (Art. III-390). This would be an improvement to the system of selection of the members of the Committee, but it would certainly be better if the national and European bodies concerned were more involved in the establishment of the list of the members.

4.6.4. What is the structure and what are the functions of the Committee of the Regions?

The Treaty establishing the European Community officially acknowledges the regional diversity and the role played by regions in the governance of the Community through the Committee of the Regions made up of **representatives of regional and local bodies** (Art. 263-265 TEC). The 317 members of the Committee and an equal number of alternate members (with the same national distribution as the members of the ESC) are proposed by the governments of the Member States and appointed for four years by the Council, acting unanimously.

The Committee of the Regions **must be consulted** by the Council or the Commission on matters relating notably to employment guidelines, legislation on social matters, environment, education, vocational training, culture, public health, European networks and the Structural Funds. It **may be consulted** in all other cases considered appropriate by one of the two institutions, in particular those which concern cross-border cooperation. It can also issue an **own-initiative opinion** when it considers that specific regional interests are at stake (Art. 265 TEC). The Committee of the Regions thus involves regional and local authorities in the decision-making process and expresses their views on all common policies concerning them. Yet again, these views could have a greater impact on these policies than they now have, if a way was found to make the decision-making organs to take them more seriously into consideration.

As in the case of the Economic and Social Committee, the **Constitutional Treaty** only lengthens the term of office of the members of the Committee of the Regions to five years, limits their maximum number to 350 and stipulates that the Committee's composition would be determined by the Council acting unanimously on a proposal from the Commission (Art. III-386). However, the Constitution does not encourage the Council to obtain the opinion of the regional and local bodies concerned nor does it elevate the importance of the opinions of the Committee of the Regions.

Chapter 5

EUROPEAN LEGISLATION

Common policies, which are the essential element of multinational integration [see section 1.3.1], are based on **common legislation**. Inherent in the concept of a common policy is its **binding force on the member states**. The latter must give the common institutions the legal means to implement common policies and to enforce their decisions on all the parties concerned and on their citizens. Hence, common policies are shaped by legal acts agreed by the common institutions, implemented by the member states and/or the common institutions and controlled by the common institutions. The national laws of the member states are harmonised in a great number of fields in the context of common policies.

A special law, based on the treaties and called acquis communautaire, is thus built to bring into being common policies, a law that is superimposed and takes **precedence over national law**, even the constitutional law, of the Member States, whether national legislation predates or postdates Community legislation. In fact, the Member States have definitively transferred sovereign rights to the Community they created, and they cannot subsequently go back on that transfer through unilateral measures, unless they decide to break away from the EC/EU [see section 3.3.2]. If they do not opt for such a radical measure, they cannot contravene European legislation, to the making of which they have contributed, by invoking their national, even their constitutional law. Several judgements of the European Court of Justice have established this principle. This is another feature of the multinational integration process, which distinguishes it from intergovernmental cooperation, where decisions may have political consequences but do not carry a legal binding force on the participating states [see section 1.2.1]. A multinational integration process, such as that of the EC/EU, could not function, if each Member State could circumvent the common legislation by bringing into play its national - including its constitutional - law.

5.1. The legislative competences of the Community

5.1.1. Why do the Member States confer legislative competences to the EC/EU?

The European Community/Union is not a federal state but brings together nation-states via the process of multinational integration. The powers assigned to the Community by the Treaties are supplementary to those of its Member States. The Community can act in an area only in so far as the competence has been conferred to it by the Member States (principle of conferral) [see section 3.3.2]. Very few areas come under exclusive European competence. Accordingly, nearly all **common policies have a European dimension and a national dimension** [see section 3.3.3]. The appropriate decision-making level - national, European or both simultaneously - depends on the type of each policy measure under consideration. In the case of laws or decisions which must apply uniformly in all Member States, there is little room for national initiative. On the contrary, when the Treaty provides for non-binding coordination of national policies, the scale of European action leaves a wide margin of manoeuvre to the national authorities. As a common policy develops, the European dimension increases at the expense of the national dimension [see section 1.3.4]. The Member States accept the decrease of their powers to the extent that their interests are better served by common action than by national action [see sections 1.3.4 and 6.2.8].

When the member states of a multinational integration scheme adopt a fundamental or secondary common policy, they implicitly recognise that it has an added value in relation to their previously independent national policies in a certain field. The very existence of a common policy is due to the fact that it has the potential of better achieving the goals of the member states than the individual national policies pursued in disarray [see section 1.3.3]. In other words, common policies exist because the member states appreciate their advantages. The main drawback compared with the expected benefits of the common policies developed by multinational integration is a certain loss of national sovereignty, due to the commitments accepted by the member states. Certainly, the states which opt for the integration process lose some of their independence in terms of goals and means of their national policies, since segments of their national sovereignties are blended into a new concept of **"shared sovereignty" that is intended to serve better their various national interests**. But, this loss of independence is circumscribed by two means: the continuing influence of the member states in the development of the common policies after their inception, through the common institutions in which they participate [see section 5.2.4]; and the possibility left to the member states to choose the means that are best suited to attain the common goals of the common policies, by virtue of the principles of subsidiarity and proportionality [see sections 5.1.2 and 5.1.3].

The **Constitutional Treaty** does not depart from current practice on the question of transfer of sovereign rights from the Member States to the Union, but it defines in detail the principles which govern this transfer and guarantees that these principles should not be infringed [see section 3.3.2]. According to the Constitution, these principles are: the principle of conferral of competences (Art. I-11); the clear distinction of the Union's competences into areas of exclusive competence, of shared competence and of support of national policies (Art. I-13 to I-17); and the exercise of these competences in accordance with the principles of subsidiarity and proportionality under the control of national parliaments.

5.1.2. What is the meaning of the principle of subsidiarity?

The **principle of subsidiarity** means that the Community must not undertake or regulate what can be managed or regulated more efficiently at national or regional levels. This principle, implying multi-level governance, must be exercised in a spirit of cooperation between the various levels of power. According to the Treaties (Art. 2 TEU and art. 5 TEC), the Community must act within the limits of the powers conferred upon it by the Treaties and of the objectives assigned to it therein [see section 3.3.2]. In areas which do not fall within its exclusive competence, the Community must take action, in accordance with the principle of subsidiarity, only if and in so far as the objectives of the proposed action cannot be sufficiently achieved by the Member States and can therefore, by reason of the scale or effects of the proposed action, be better achieved by the Community. Any action by the Community must not go beyond what is necessary to achieve the objectives of the Treaties. Article 308 of the EC Treaty enables the Council, by unanimity and after consulting the European Parliament, to introduce the provisions needed to attain a common objective, but does not make it possible to create new powers for the Community.

The Commission applies the principle of subsidiarity both to direct its initiatives and to evaluate the need for Community legislation, both future and existing. It conducts wide-ranging consultations and presents whenever necessary reference documents (Green Papers) prior to proposing legislative texts. In the explanatory memorandum accompanying its proposals, the Commission includes a "subsidiarity recital" summarising the objectives of the proposed measure, its effectiveness and why it is necessary. The Council verifies that a proposal of the Commission is in accordance with the provisions of Article 5 (TEC), on the basis of the preamble and the explanatory memorandum of the proposal.

5.1.3. What is the meaning of the principle of proportionality?

The principle of proportionality implies that, if a Community action proves to be necessary to attain the objectives of the Treaty, the Community institutions must further **examine whether legislative action is required** or whether other sufficiently effective means can be used (financial support, encouragement of cooperation between Member States by a Recommendation, inducement to take action by a Resolution, etc.).

To comply with the principle of proportionality, Community action must be as simple as possible, consistent with satisfactory achievement of its objectives. The Community must therefore **legislate only to the extent necessary** and give preference to directives rather than regulations and to framework directives rather than detailed measures [see section 5.3.1]. Moreover, Community measures must leave as much scope for national decision as possible; and respect well established national arrangements and the working of Member States legal systems. The important thing is to ensure that Community legislation does not impose on national, regional or local authorities or on civil society any constraints which are illogical, superfluous or excessive given the objective.

5.1.4. What is the status of Community law?

The status of the Community law is a unique one, in that its application depends, by and large, on the separate jurisdictions of the Member States. The Community does not seek a total legal harmonisation, which would eliminate the distinctive features of national jurisdictions. However, both the European institutions and the Member States have a duty to **ensure that Community law is**

respected and to take the necessary steps when it is violated. This is a fundamental requirement of any legal system. The authorities of Member States, including the courts, must ensure compliance with the principle of uniform interpretation of directives, in the light of their wording and purpose. In case of conflict of laws, the national judge must, according to the European Court, not apply any contrary clauses of the national law, whether these are prior or subsequent to Community law [see section 4.5.2].

One characteristic common to the Treaties establishing the European Communities is that they are not conventional international treaties which create rights and obligations for the States alone. These Treaties and the legislation derived from them engender rights and obligations not only for the Member States but also for their nationals. This **"direct effect" of Community law** means notably that any person may ask his judge to apply the Community law which contradicts the national law. Citizens may thus invoke Community law before national courts and, if necessary, before the Court of Justice of the European Communities. According to the Court, a Member State is obliged to make good damage caused to individuals, even where the national legislature is responsible for a breach of Community law. An individual can apply for the annulment of a decision, a regulation and even a directive of a general legislative nature, if he can prove that he is directly and individually affected by its provisions.

5.2. The Community decision-making procedure

5.2.1. What is the Community method of decision-making?

The "Community method" of decision-making is provided by the original European Treaties and actually by the Treaty establishing the European Community (TEC) [see chapter 3]. This method entails the following elements: (a) a single and supranational source of the right of initiative; (b) usually co-decision of the European Parliament with the Council, deciding by qualified majority; and (c) control of the decisions by a supranational judicial authority, the European Court of Justice. The Community method is, indeed, an **original combination of: technocratic proposals** emanating from the Commission, worked out with the technical advice of experts from all the Member States; **and legislative acts and political decisions** taken by the Council, representing the governments of the Member States, usually in tandem with the European Parliament, representing the peoples of the Union [see section 5.2.4].

The Community method does not imply legislation by the European Commission. The Community Treaties authorise the Commission to propose legislative acts and to execute the legislative and other decisions taken by the legislative bodies [see section 4.2.2]. The rhetoric about the "decisions taken by the technocrats of Brussels" (meaning the Commission) is maliciously erroneous. The fact is that the technocrats propose the Community measures; but it is the political institutions representing the democratically elected governments (the Council of Ministers) and the citizens of the Member States (the European Parliament) that take the decisions. Except in a few areas, such as competition, where the Treaties give it full competence, the Commission may only adopt acts implementing the decisions of the legislative bodies.

5.2.2. Why does the Commission have the initiative of proposal?

The Member States have empowered the Commission with the initiative for the Community's decision-making procedure because they consider it as **an independent arbitrator of their various national interests**. Therefore, the Community Treaties authorise the Commission to prepare all proposals for Parliament and/or Council Regulations, Directives and Decisions. The Commission's role is political in so far as it chooses and prepares the ground on which the construction of the Community is undertaken, but otherwise its role is technocratic as its proposals are based on technical considerations and/or scientific grounds. Using an "impact assessment method", the Commission analyses the direct and indirect implications of a proposed measure (e.g. concerning businesses, trade, employment, the environment and health). The results of each assessment are made public.

Moreover, the Commission is **responsible for defining in its proposals the common interest** or the interest of the Community. To make sure that its proposal is adopted, the Commission must take into consideration the often-divergent interests of the Member States and endeavour to detect and express the common interest. If it does not succeed in this definition or if it does not itself amend its proposal, taking into consideration the positions of the other Community organs, all the Member States together, in total agreement within the Council, must find a different definition of the common interest inherent in a proposal of a common policy or a common measure (Art. 250 TEC); something that happens very rarely.

5.2.3. How can the Commission determine the common interest of the Member States?

The Commission must define the common interest in each Community initiative, because it is entrusted by the Community Treaties - hence, by the Member States - with the role of a supranational and independent arbitrator set above the individual national interests. In fact, the Commission can play this role, thanks to two main characteristic elements: its supranational nature; and its technocratic approach to problems and their solutions.

The **supranational nature** of the Commission is due to two intertwined elements. Firstly, it is made up of politicians (at its top) and technocrats (at its base) of all nationalities [see section 4.2.1]. Secondly, it is controlled by no one national authority, but by multinational organs: the European Council, the European Parliament and the European Court of Justice. The multinational composition of the college of Commissioners and of the services which work under them means that no one of the officials (often called Eurocrats) or even of the Commissioners can influence a proposal that he or she is working on in the direction of the national interest of one or some Member State(s). If he or she tried to do so, he or she would immediately be called to order by his or her colleagues in the responsible service or in the collegiate body of the Commission.

The **technocratic approach of the initiatives of the Commission** means that its services, which are organised in a similar way as national Ministries, are advised by specialised committees of experts, established by the Council or the Commission itself. These committees are made up of scientific, technical, administrative and professional experts from all the Member States. These advisory committees examine a problem from its technical, economic and legal aspects and analyse the pros and cons of all possible solutions, including the inaction of the Community/Union. The Commission listens to all views and arguments, expressed in the various committees, and usually takes up in its proposal the majority views, believing that upon them can be built a consensus in the decision-making bodies, the European Parliament and the Council. After all, the Commission knows well that, in order for any one of its proposals to have a chance to be adopted by these bodies, it has to fulfil the common interest of all the Member States or of the large majority of them.

Of course, the Commission is not infallible and it may sometimes be mistaken in the evaluation of what is the best solution in the interest of all or most Member States. Therefore, **many subsequent controls** exist, which make it possible to assess and eventually correct a proposal of the Commission. At the same time as it is sent to the decision-making bodies, the proposal of the Commission is, in many cases, sent to the advisory bodies set up by the Treaty: the Economic and Social Committee, consisting of representatives of the various economic and social components of organised civil society, and in particular representatives of producers, farmers, carriers, workers, dealers, craftsmen, professional occupations, consumers and the general interest (Art. 257 TEC) [see section 4.6.3]; and the Committee of the Regions, consisting of representatives of regional and local bodies who either hold a regional or local authority electoral mandate or are politically accountable to an elected assembly (Art. 263 TEC) [see section 4.6.4]. These bodies examine the employment, social, environmental, regional and other impacts of a Commission proposal and give their opinion to the decision-making bodies.

All these administrative, scientific, technical and national filters through which passes a proposal of the Commission and its eventual amendments ensure that this is the closest possible to the common interest and to the best possible solution at the time of its conception. In any case, the ultimate judges of the soundness of the Commission's definition of the **best solution in the common interest of the Member States** are the decision-making bodies: the European Parliament and the Council [see section 5.2.4]. These bodies have their own multinational committees, which discuss at length all Commission proposals, particularly from the point of view of the various national interests involved in the problem and in its proposed solution. Their opinions weigh heavily in the deliberations of the plenary assembly of the Parliament and of the Ministers sitting in the responsible Council configuration. These discussions often take many months or even years and usually result in many amendments to the original proposal of the Commission. Even if a nationally biased or otherwise discriminatory proposal passed through all the tests of the advisory and decision-making organs, it could be brought before the Court of Justice for annulment by any Member State believing that it violated the word or the spirit of the Treaty [see section 4.5.2].

5.2.4. What is the co-decision procedure of the Parliament with the Council?

The European Parliament is ever more involved in the Community decision-making process under two procedures, co-decision and cooperation with the Council of Ministers. Article 251 (TEC), defines the **co-decision procedure** of the Council with the European Parliament. This procedure was introduced by the Treaty of Maastricht and was largely extended by the Amsterdam and Nice amendments of the TEC [see section 3.2]. It is now applied to practically all important matters covered by this Treaty, including the implementation of the freedoms of the internal market, social policy, environment policy and consumer protection.

In the co-decision procedure, the Council acting by a qualified majority [see section 5.2.6] adopts "common positions", which may be accepted, rejected or amended by the Parliament. If the Council does not agree with the amendments proposed by the Parliament, a **conciliation committee**, composed of equal numbers of representatives of the two institutions, must bring together the different points of view. The Commission can act as an arbitrator between the two decision-making bodies, by accepting in its amended proposal some of the amendments proposed by the Parliament.

In the rare cases where a compromise solution is not found, the Parliament may reject the proposed act by absolute majority of expressed votes. Thus, **the Parliament has the final word** in this legislative procedure. Regulations, Directives and Decisions [see section 5.3.1] adopted under the co-decision procedure are signed both by the President of the European Parliament and the President of the Council. The co-decision procedure has worked well so far. Indeed decisions have been taken fairly quickly as a result of a good working relationship between the institutions.

The **Constitutional Treaty** stipulates that European laws and framework laws [see section 5.3.3] shall be adopted, on the basis of proposals from the Commission, jointly by the European Parliament and the Council under the **ordinary legislative procedure**. This procedure is modelled on the actual co-decision procedure and on the conciliation procedure related to it (Art. III-396). The scope of the ordinary legislative procedure is, however, considerably extended, thus giving the Parliament equal legislative powers with the Council of Ministers in practically all areas of the Union's activities, including the adoption of the budget, but excluding the common foreign and security policy [see section 6.4.8].

5.2.5. What about the democratic deficit of the Community?

On the basis of the original Treaties, the Council was the only legislative authority of the Community and this was the main reason for the then existing democratic deficit of the Community. Subsequent amendments of the Treaties [see chapter 3] have joined, ever more closely, the European Parliament in the decision-making process, thus making the Council one of the two legislative authorities and **reducing, consequently, the democratic deficit** [see sections 4.3.2 and 5.2.4]. Going a step further, the Constitutional Treaty specifies that the Council shall, jointly with the European Parliament, exercise legislative and budgetary functions (Art. I-23). Hence, the legislative functions of the Council will resemble those of an Upper House or Senate, representing the governments of the Member States and those of the European Parliament will be similar to the functions of a national parliament.

In fact, European **citizens already have almost the same influence** on the shaping of European law as they have on the shaping of national law. They indirectly influence it through the choice of the political parties, which make up the national governments and which therefore are involved in all European decisions adopted by the Council of Ministers [see section 4.4.1]. In addition, citizens have a direct say in the election of the members of the European Parliament [see section 4.3.1], which has an important participation in the legislative process, thanks to improvements brought by successive European Treaties. It follows that **the "democratic deficit" of the Community is another myth** propagated by eurosceptic circles. Paradoxically, these same circles are among the most vehement detractors of the Constitutional Treaty, which would practically eliminate the remnants of the democratic deficit as far as the matters covered by the actual Community Treaty are concerned [see section 3.3.4]. They also oppose the application of the Community method to the subjects covered by the European Union Treaty, where a democratic deficit really exists [see section 6.4].

The **Constitutional Treaty** defines, for the first time, the democratic foundations of the Union, which are based on three principles: those of democratic equality, representative democracy and participatory democracy. The principle of **democratic equality** means that all citizens of the Union must receive equal attention from its institutions, bodies, offices and agencies (Art. I-45). The principle of **representative democracy** means that citizens are directly represented at Union level in the European Parliament, while Member States are represented in the European Council by their

Heads of State or Government and in the Council by their governments, themselves democratically accountable either to their national parliaments, or to their citizens (Art. I-46). The principle of **participatory democracy** means that the institutions must give citizens and representative associations the opportunity to make known and publicly exchange their views in all areas of Union action (Art I-47). The main innovation in this area is that one million citizens who are nationals of a significant number of Member States may take the initiative of inviting the Commission to submit any appropriate proposal on matters where citizens consider that a legal act of the Union is required. This right of initiative gives those European citizens who complain about the "democratic deficit in Europe" a means of directly making their voices heard.

5.2.6. What is qualified majority voting in the Council?

At present, where the Treaties do not provide otherwise, the Council takes decisions by a simple majority of its members. This is rarely the case, however, as in the vast majority of instances the Treaties provide that decisions are taken either by unanimity or by qualified majority. Unanimity is undemocratic, because the vote of the smallest country weighs as much as that of the largest and any country can block a decision wished by all its other partners. To curb unanimity voting, the amendments of the Treaties have extended qualified majority voting, notably in the areas where there is participation of the Parliament in the decision-making process [see section 5.2.4]. **Qualified majority** is calculated on the basis of votes allocated to each Member State under Article 205 (TEC), as modified by the Accession Act of the ten new Member States. According to the latter, the total number of votes in the Council is 321 and is distributed to the 25 Ministers in a weighted manner, so that the influence of a Member State in the decision-making process is more or less related to the size of its population. Actually, **the votes of the Council members are weighted as follows**:

- Germany, France, Italy and the United Kingdom 29 each;
- Spain and Poland 27 each;
- Netherlands 13;
- Belgium, the Czech Republic, Greece, Hungary and Portugal 12 each;
- Austria and Sweden 10 each;
- Denmark, Finland, Ireland, Lithuania and Slovakia 7 each;
- Cyprus, Estonia, Latvia, Luxembourg and Slovenia 4 each; and
- Malta 3.

As a rule, decisions taken by qualified majority on the basis of a Commission proposal must gather at least **72% of the total votes of the members (i.e. 232 votes), representing at least 62% of the total population** of the Union. The same conditions apply to Article 34 of the EU Treaty, but the 232 votes in favour should, in any case, be cast by at least two-thirds of the members. Whilst the qualified-majority voting system of the Treaty of Nice technically opened the door to enlargement, the weighting of the votes in the Council in no way improves the efficiency and transparency of the decision-making process, a fact which gives cause for serious concern as to how it may operate in a Union of 27 or more Member States.

Responding to this concern, **the Constitutional Treaty**, firstly, generalises qualified majority voting in the ordinary legislative procedure [see section 5.2.4]. Secondly, it abandons the weighting of the votes in the Council and, thus, simplifies greatly the system of qualified majority, applicable from November 2009. In effect, Article I-25 of the Constitution defines qualified majority as at least **55% of the members** of the Council or the European Council (72%, if the Council is not acting on a proposal of the Commission or of the Union Minister for Foreign Affairs), comprising at least fifteen of them (i.e. 60% of the 25) and representing **at least 65% of the population of the Union**. Since, at the date of the application of the new system, i.e. after the European elections of 2009, the Union will probably number 27 members, the criterion of 15 States in favour of a decision will be automatically met and will therefore become obsolete. In fact, in a Union of more than 25 members, 55% of the total will comprise de facto 15 of them.

With the **constitutional system**, equality of Member States is respected as each one has one vote in respect of the first criterion, whilst their different population sizes are taken into account in meeting the second criterion. Council decision-making is facilitated as a greater number of combinations of Member States can constitute a qualified majority compared to the system prescribed by the Treaty of Nice. In the enlarged Union, this is essential for its ability to act and for the smooth operation of its institutions. Moreover, according to Article I-25, a blocking minority must include at least four Member States, so as to preclude three "big" Member States, representing more than 35% of the Union's population, from forming an alliance to block a decision. Last but not least, the constitutional system, which defines once and for all the criteria of qualified majority, would prevent, during subsequent enlargements, long negotiations on the allocation of votes to Member States and the definition of the qualified majority threshold.

5.2.7. What is enhanced cooperation of some Member States?

So as to prevent one or two Member States from blocking further progress of the Union in certain fields, the Treaty of Nice has reinforced and facilitated **enhanced cooperations**, which aim at safeguarding the values and serving the interests of the Union as a whole by asserting its identity as a coherent force on the international scene (Art. 27a to 28 and 40 to 45 (TEU) and 11 (TEC). **In connection with the EC Treaty**, the veto possibility is removed. Member States which intend to establish enhanced cooperation between themselves must address a request to the Commission, which should submit a proposal to the Council to that effect or inform the Member States concerned of the reasons for not doing so. The assent of the European Parliament is required for an enhanced cooperation in a field coming under the co-decision procedure (Art 11 TEC). **In connection with the common foreign and security policy (CFSP)**, enhanced cooperation is possible for the implementation of a joint action or common position [see section 6.4.5], except in the sphere of the security and defence policy (Art 27b TEU) [see section 6.4.7]. The Council should act by qualified majority [see section 5.2.6], but the 232 votes in favour of the decision should be cast by at least two-thirds of the members (Art. 23.2 TEU).

The Constitutional Treaty does not change much the rules concerning enhanced cooperation, a cooperation which **should aim to further the objectives of the Union**, protect its interests and reinforce its integration process. Such cooperation should be open at any time to all Member States (Articles I-44 and III-416 to III-423). In the field of CFSP, the European decision authorising enhanced cooperation should be adopted by the Council, acting unanimously, as a last resort, when it has established that the objectives of such cooperation could not be attained within a reasonable period by the Union as a whole, and provided that at least one third of the Member States participate in it.

However, the conditions enabling certain Member States to establish an enhanced cooperation may be difficult to obtain and some are even liable to subjective and hence questionable definitions, in particular the condition that an enhanced cooperation respects the competences, rights and obligations of the Member States which do not participate in it (Art. III-417). It should be said that, until now, enhanced cooperations have either been inscribed in the Treaty (participation in the euro-zone) or have been consecrated by it a posteriori (Schengen cooperation agreement).

5.3. The Community legal system

5.3.1. Which are the legal acts actually used by the European Community?

The legal acts, which substantiate the common policies, may be undertaken by the competent institutions with legal effect only if they are empowered to do so by the European Treaties (principle of conferral or of attribution of powers) [see section 3.3.2]. Article 249 of the EC Treaty provides for five forms of legal act, each with a different effect on the Member States' legal systems. Some are directly applicable in place of national legislation, while others permit the progressive adjustment of that legislation to Community provisions.

The **regulation** has a general scope, is binding in all its elements and is directly applicable in each Member State. Just like a national law, it gives rise to rights and obligations directly applicable to the citizens of the European Union. The regulation substitutes European law for national law and is therefore the most effective legal instrument provided for by the EC Treaty. As "European laws", regulations must be complied with fully by those to whom they are addressed (individuals, Member States, European institutions).

The **directive** binds any Member State to which it is addressed with regard to the result to be achieved, while allowing the national authorities competency as to the form and methods used. It is a sort of Community framework law and lends itself particularly well to the harmonisation of national laws. It defines the objective or objectives to be attained by a common policy and leaves it to the Member States to choose the forms and instruments necessary for complying with it. Since the Member States are only bound by the objectives laid down in directives, they have some discretion, in transposing them into national law, to take into account special national circumstances. They must, however, adopt the national measures necessary for implementation of the Directive within time-limits set by it, failing which they are infringing Community legislation.

The **decision** is binding on the addressees it indicates, who may be one, several, or even all the Member States or one or more natural or legal persons. This variety of potential addressees is coupled with a variety in the scope of its contents, which may extend from a quasi regulation or a quasi directive to a specific administrative decision. In any case, according to the Court of Justice, a decision can produce direct effects creating for the individuals rights that national jurisdictions must safeguard.

The above legal acts are binding on the Member States, the Community institutions and, in many cases, the citizens of the Member States. They constitute the Community law and are published in the "L" series (legislation) of the Official Journal of the European Union (OJ). The Official Journal is published every day in all the official languages of the Community/Union and is freely available in the electronic database EUR-Lex of the Europa server of the Commission (http://europa.eu.int/eur-lex/en/index.html.).

5.3.2. Which are the non-binding instruments of the EC/EU?

In addition to common legislation, the objectives of the common policies are sometimes sought by **non-binding concerted action**, taking the form of coordination of national policies, mechanisms for exchanging information, bodies for cooperation, Community programmes and/or financial support [see section 1.2.2].

Therefore, in addition to the above binding acts, the Council and the Commission can adopt **Recommendations** suggesting a certain line of conduct or outlining the goals of a common policy and **opinions** assessing a current situation or certain facts in the Community or the Member States. Furthermore, the Council and the European Parliament adopt **Resolutions**, which are also not binding, suggesting a political desire to act in a given area. These instruments enable the Community institutions to suggest guidelines for coordination of national legislations or administrative practices in a non-binding manner, i.e. without any legal obligations for the addressees - Member States and/or citizens.

While Resolutions and opinions are published in the "C" series (communications) of the Official Journal of the European Union, recommendations are published in the "L" series (legislation) of the OJ, in order to stress their political importance. The same is true for the **common positions** and **joint actions** of the common foreign and security policy and of justice and home affairs (Art. 12 31 of TEU). They are published in the L series of the OJ, although they have not a legal binding force on the Member States. They embody, however, political commitments for joint behaviour and/or action.

5.3.3. Which are the legal acts proposed by the Constitutional Treaty?

The Constitutional Treaty **renames and simplifies the legal instruments of the Union**. After its coming into force, the institutions will adopt European laws, European framework laws, European regulations, European decisions, recommendations and opinions (Art. I-33).

A **European law** will be a legislative act of general application, binding in its entirety and directly applicable in all Member States (like the present regulation). A **European framework law** will be a legislative act binding, as to the result to be achieved, but will leave to the national authorities the choice of form and methods (like the current directive). The European laws and framework laws will be adopted by the European Parliament and the Council in accordance with the ordinary legislative procedure (Art. I-34) [see section 5.2.4]. A **European regulation** will be a non-legislative act of general application for the implementation of legislative acts and will have the binding force and applicability of the main act. A **European decision** will be a non-legislative act, either binding in its entirety or binding only those to whom it is addressed. The European Council may adopt decisions, the Council, the Commission and the European Central Bank may adopt regulations and decisions (Art. I-35).

Recommendations - usually adopted by the Council and in specific cases by the Commission or the European Central Bank - and **opinions** - usually adopted by the advisory Committees [see sections 4.6.3 and 4.6.4] - will have no binding force.

5.4. The Community financial system

The conventional international organisations such as the United Nations or the Organisation for Economic Cooperation and Development (OECD) are financed by contributions from their member countries. In most instances their financial requirements amount to staff and operational expenditure: if they are entrusted with operational tasks, their financing is generally provided on an "à la carte" basis by those member countries which agreed on those tasks. It is virtually never a question, in such organisations, of financial transfers or even of financial compensation. The European Community, on the other hand, although it is not a federation in the formal sense, pursues many federating common policies, which call for a **transfer of resources from the national to the supranational level** [see section 1.1.].

5.4.1. Why does the Community need its own budget?

Some common policies of the European Community/Union are clearly in the interest of the stronger and wealthier Member States. This is the case notably of the internal market, competition and taxation policies, because they open the markets of the weaker and poorer Member States to their products and services [see sections 6.1.3 and 6.2.3]. Therefore, some other policies are needed to **balance the benefits of the integration process**, by operating capital transfers in favour of the poorer Member States: e.g. agricultural, regional and social policies. These transfers of capital are also in the interest of the wealthier Member States, since they allow their poorer partners to buy more of their products and services. This balance of the benefits of the Member States, which distinguishes, *inter alia*, a multinational integration scheme from a free trade area one [see section 1.2.1], is organised by the Community budget.

The implementation of many common policies requires, indeed, not only legal but also some financial means. Certainly, not all common policies need common financing. For example, competition and taxation policies are based almost exclusively on legal measures. But the implementation of most common policies is based on a mixture of legal and financial measures. Common regional, education, aid to development policies, e.g., would be seriously restrained without Community financing of their common programmes. There could be no common agricultural or fisheries policies, in the sense that we know them, without common support of prices and/or incomes. It is a political value judgment whether there should be more or less common financing of this or that common policy and this judgment is subject to a long debate carried out every year among the budgetary authorities of the Community [see section 5.4.3]. The result of this multinational political debate is recorded in the **Community budget**.

5.4.2. Which are the own resources of the Community?

In the beginning of the European Economic Community, the contribution of the Member States to the Community budget was determined on a scale according to Gross National Product (GNP) shares or other criteria. Provision had been made in the EEC Treaty for replacing the Member States' initial contributions by **own resources** after establishment of the Common Customs Tariff (CCT) [see section 6.1.5]. The transfer of customs revenue to the Community budget was a logical upshot of the realisation of a genuine customs union [see section 6.1.2]. In such a union the country of import of goods from a third country is not always the country of final destination of those goods. The revenue from **customs duties** is therefore often collected in a country other than the country of destination or of consumption. Only the payment of that revenue to the customs union, in this instance to the Community, makes it possible to neutralise such a tax collecting paradox. This is, moreover, an important integrating element, which again differentiates a customs union from a free trade area [see section 1.2.1].

However, since the realisation of the customs union in 1968, the importance of customs duties was continually diminishing inasmuch as they were being progressively abolished or reduced under the General Agreement on Tariffs and Trade (GATT) and the various tariff concessions granted to the least developed countries. For that reason it was decided, in 1970, to use a proportion of the **value added tax (VAT)** as an additional source of Community financing. That tax, which has a uniform basis of assessment, takes fairly accurate account of the economic capacity of the citizens of the Member States, as it is levied at the consumption level. The "**uniform base**", which was adopted for calculating the proportion (actually 0,5%) of the VAT yield which each country must pay to the EU, is made up of all taxable supplies of goods and provisions of services in the Union. Hence, the harmonisation achieved thanks to the common taxation policy has had an important side effect on the financing of other common policies.

5.4.3. Which are the budgetary authorities of the Community?

The Community budget is decided every year by politicians from the Member States sitting in the Council and the European Parliament on the basis of technical reports and proposals provided by the Commission. According to the **actual budgetary procedure**, the Commission prepares a preliminary draft Community budget, which it submits to the Council. The Council then adopts a draft budget based on the Commission's draft and forwards it to the Parliament for a first reading.

The Parliament, by means of amendments, can propose modifications that do not increase the total volume of the budget concerning "**compulsory expenditure**" (CE), i.e. expenditure resulting from the Treaties and the decisions adopted pursuant thereto (roughly 50% of appropriations, made up chiefly of those relating to the common agricultural policy). Moreover, the Parliament can propose increases, up to a maximum level, for the **"non-compulsory" category of expenditure**, i.e. expenditure which is not the automatic consequence of the various Community provisions (in particular, appropriations allocated to the European Social Fund, research, energy, etc.). The Council acts on these amendments and proposed modifications by qualified majority [see section 5.2.6] and returns the draft budget to the Parliament for a second reading. At the end of the second reading, the Parliament can either adopt the budget or reject it en bloc, in which case it is necessary to begin the procedure afresh through the submission of new proposals by the Commission.

Going a step further, the **Constitutional Treaty** jointly vests the Parliament and the Council with budgetary as with legislative functions (Art. I-23). The differentiation of the budgetary powers of the Parliament between compulsory and non-compulsory expenditure is abolished by the Constitution. The law determining the annual budget of the Union will be adopted jointly by the EP and the Council, **with the Parliament having the final word on the budget** as a whole (Art. III-404). Thus, if the Constitution came into force, the European Parliament would have practically the same budgetary functions as a national parliamentary assembly.

5.4.4. How is the Community budget managed and how is controlled?

The **management of the Community budget is entrusted to the Commission** (Art. 274 TEC) [see section 4.2.3] and is exercised according to a Financial Regulation, which sets the principles and ground rules governing the establishment and implementation of the budget and financial control. Like other public funds, the European Union budget runs the risk of having fraudsters enrich themselves at its expense or embezzle the levies which normally should be transferred to the Union. Therefore, the management of the Community budget is subject to several controls.

The **Court of Auditors examines the accounts** of all revenue and expenditure of the Community [see section 4.6.2], particularly the annual budget managed by the Commission, and of all bodies set up by the Community. It examines in particular whether all revenue has been received and all expenditure incurred in a lawful and regular manner and must report on any cases of irregularity (Art. 248 TEC). Moreover, the Commission is **officially controlled by the European Parliament**, which, on a recommendation from the Council, gives it a discharge in respect of the implementation of the budget (Art. 276 TEC). If the Parliament disapproves the management of the Community budget by the Commission, it can pronounce a vote of censure against it and force it to resign.

However, the **fight against fraud cannot be led from Brussels alone**. Indeed, roughly 80% of expenditure is handled by tens of thousands of national, regional or local officials. Responsibility for ensuring that the funds are properly used rests, therefore, with the national authorities in the first place and it is essential that complementary action be developed at Union level through close cooperation between the Member States and the Commission. Therefore, Article 280 of the EC Treaty stipulates that the Member States must **coordinate their action aimed at protecting the financial interests of the Community** against fraud and must take the same measures to counter fraud affecting the financial interests of the Community as they take to counter fraud affecting their own financial interests.

Chapter 6

THE STAGES OF INTEGRATION

Although the multinational integration process is continuous [see section 1.1], **four large stages may be distinguished**: customs union, common market, economic and monetary union and, finally, political union. Such distinction is useful, not only for analytical purposes, but because the passage from one stage to the other necessitates a fundamental decision of the participating member states to transfer new parcels of sovereignty from national to supranational level, sanctioned by treaty agreed by their governments and parliaments [see chapter 3]. The EC/EU is clearly following this evolutionary pattern.

In the isolationist period, usually following a devastating war, like the Second World War, states erect **high protection barriers against foreign trade** and therefore against international competition. These may be customs barriers (tariffs, quotas and measures having equivalent effect), fiscal barriers (higher levels of taxation for goods largely manufactured outside the country), administrative barriers (complicated bureaucratic procedures for imports) or technical barriers (concerning, for example, environment or human health protection) serving in one way or another to discourage or even prohibit imports. This is the zero point in the scale of multinational integration.

Totalitarian regimes apart, such a protectionist system cannot last for long. It leads to **great dissatisfaction on the part of consumers**, whose choice is very restricted, and on the part of the most dynamic and/or **less protected businessmen**, who find their field of activity limited by the barriers. Dissatisfied citizens, as consumers and voters, and progressive businessmen, as influential interest groups, press the political elite to reduce external protection. Under the *sine qua non* condition that the latter would be susceptible to such pressures and would sincerely be seeking the maximisation of national interests - two prerequisites that exclude authoritarian regimes - they would normally start discussing the possibilities of trade liberalisation with like-minded elite in neighbouring countries. Indeed, by its very nature, trade liberalisation cannot be decided unilaterally but can only be envisaged in a multinational context. However, if the economic and political elite of several states were to agree on the desirability of mutual trade liberalisation, they would still have an option: to pursue it with intergovernmental cooperation, in a free trade area, or with a multinational integration process in a customs union [see section 1.2].

6.1. The customs union stage

6.1.1. What is the difference between a customs union and a free trade area?

A **free trade area** is based on intergovernmental cooperation [see section 1.2.1]. In such an area, member countries abolish import duties and other customs barriers to the free movement of goods manufactured in the territory of their partners [see section 2.2.1]. However, each country **retains its own external tariff and its customs policy** vis-à-vis third countries. It also retains entirely its national sovereignty. Compared to isolationism, trade liberalisation is a common policy of a group of states, but, since without concessions of sovereignty, there can be no spillover from this unique common policy to other policy areas [see section 1.3], a free trade area should be placed at a low level of multinational integration, before the commencement of the evolutionary process.

By contrast, in a **customs union**, which is the first stage of the evolutionary multinational integration process, free movement concerns not only products manufactured in the territory of the partners, but all products, irrespective of origin, situated in the territory of the member countries. Furthermore, the latter lose their customs autonomy and **apply a common external customs tariff** to third countries [see section 6.1.5]. In order to manage the common customs tariff, the members of a customs union must have a common commercial policy. In addition, trade liberalisation has in this case spillover or multiplicative effects on other common policies, notably, agricultural, taxation and competition. There is therefore, already at this stage - completed by the original six countries of the

EEC in July 1968 - some concession of segments of national sovereignty to the common institutions that run the customs union.

6.1.2. What is the customs union of the European Community?

Before the Community treaties came into force, every European country protected its national production with **customs tariffs**, preventing the import of goods at prices lower than those of the national production, and **quantitative restrictions**, preventing the import of certain products in quantities exceeding those which were necessary to satisfy local demand not covered by national production. Thus, a country would import the quantities and qualities not normally supplied by its internal production. As industry was well protected, it saw no need to make large-scale efforts to modernise or reduce production costs. The European consumer, faced with a limited choice and high prices for low quality goods, was the main victim of this **protectionism**. The customs union, limited initially to the coal and steel sectors governed by the ECSC Treaty but rapidly extended to all products and services, thanks to the EEC Treaty [see section 3.1], aimed at correcting this situation.

A customs union is **the first stage of multinational integration**, during which the member states agree, by treaty, to refrain from imposing any customs duties, charges having equivalent effect or quantitative restrictions on each other and to adopt an external common customs tariff in their relations with third countries. The common customs tariff implies not only a common customs policy but also a common foreign trade policy [see section 6.1.5]. Furthermore, the freedom of movement is applicable in a customs union regardless of the origin of goods, thus eliminating customs controls at internal borders.

The founders of the European Economic Community had, from the start, the goal not only of setting up a customs union but also a common market in which goods, services and capital could be traded freely [see section 6.2]. In economic integration, they foresaw not only a formula offering economic advantages but also the means to set up the conditions for political union in Europe. In order to achieve this, **a sound foundation was required**. Customs union was, accurately enough, such a foundation; it allowed for unprecedented trade growth in the participating Member States and the construction upon it of the entire European edifice. In fact, all the common policies of the European Community/Union would be unthinkable were they not based on customs union.

According to article 23 of the EC Treaty, the Community is based upon a customs union which covers all trade in goods and which involves the prohibition between Member States of customs duties on imports and exports and of all charges having equivalent effect, and the adoption of a common customs tariff in their relations with third countries [see section 6.1.5]. The customs union of the EC **covers "all trade in goods"**. This means that products coming from a third country can move freely within the Community if the import formalities have been complied with and any customs duties or charges having equivalent effect, which are payable, have been levied in the importing Member State (Art. 24 TEC).

Although the EEC Treaty gave the Member States the option of varying the rate of reduction of customs duties according to product (should a sector have difficulties), the reduction was constant and problem-free. The rate of **tariff dismantling** was even accelerated by two Council decisions, and completed on 1 July 1968, 18 months ahead of schedule. This demonstrates that tariff dismantling caused no major problems to the industries of the Member States, as any country's objection would have prevented the change of schedule provided by the Treaty. The States which acceded to the Community later on had a five-year transitional period to eliminate customs duties in intra-Community trade. This was also problem-free. Certainly, many of the previously protected industries were obliged to renovate or shut down, but many new industries were created or expanded on sound premises.

6.1.3. What problems remained after the abolition of customs barriers to trade?

The accelerated completion of the tariff union meant that, as of 1 July 1968, intra-Community trade in the original Member States was freed of customs duties and quantitative restrictions on imports and exports. However, **other trade obstacles,** such as charges having equivalent effect to customs duties and measures having equivalent effect to quantitative restrictions, were far from gone. The proper functioning of the tariff union required the removal of these obstacles too by the end of the transitional period (Art 10 EEC). In reality, as soon as tariff disarmament was accomplished, the "formalities wall" was raised between Member State administrations anxious to protect national production and at the same time prevent the decrease of their own functions and powers. Of course, every form, every stamp required for cross-border trade had a reason: tax collection, statistics, and customs checks aimed at preventing the import of products not conforming to national regulations, etc. But each stamp meant time and money to the Community's businesses.

A great number of those **trade barriers were hidden in regulations**, such as consumer or environment protection standards, which varied from one State to another. Their restrictive effects were often more damaging than customs duties and quantitative restrictions. Indeed, while customs barriers raised the price of imports or quantitatively limited them, various regulations could completely block the import of a product. Fortunately, such extreme cases were rather limited. However, the elimination of non-customs barriers to trade proved to be much more difficult and took three times as long as did the elimination of customs barriers.

6.1.4. How was the customs union completed?

The good results of the customs disarmament **spurred the completion of the common market**, itself needed for the completion of the customs union. Indeed, the customs union and the common market, which were the goals of the Treaty of Rome [see section 3.1.2], both suffered from the same problems and finally benefited from the same remedies. Heartened by the evident benefits of the customs union, the Community institutions under the leadership of the Commission waged a "war of attrition on formalities", which, thanks to the Single European Act of 1987, reached a successful conclusion on December 31, 1992 [see section 6.2.3].

Since January 1, 1993, no customs formalities are required for trade within the Community. The Community henceforth forms **one single border-free area** for the purposes of the movement of goods under cover of the TIR (international road transport) and ATA (temporary admission of goods) carnets. This saves a great deal of time for economic operators and thus helps cut the cost of transporting goods within the Community. The absence of duties and formalities bolsters intra-EU trade (dispatches and arrivals) which represents around 65% of the total trade of the Fifteen and up to 80% of the total imports or exports of some countries of the Union.

Also since January 1993, the **free movement of persons** provided for by Article 18 of the EC Treaty has been achieved, thanks to the abolition of border controls [see section 6.2.4]. Individuals travelling from one Member State to another pay VAT there where they purchase the goods and are **no longer subject to any VAT-related taxation or any border formality** when they cross from one Member State to another. In return, the system of travellers' allowances (tax free sales in ports, airports, etc.) was abolished in intra-Community travelling.

6.1.5. What is the Common Customs Tariff?

Apart from removing obstacles to intra-Community trade, a customs union is characterised by the existence of **a single external tariff applied by all Member States to imports coming from third countries**. Such imports only have to clear customs once and can then move freely within the common customs area. Reaching an agreement among the original Member States [see section 2.1] on a single external tariff required a complex striking of balances and compromises, given the different national interests, stemming from the different products that each country wished to protect. The **Common Customs Tariff (CCT)** adopted by the European institutions in 1968 is, therefore, a major achievement of European integration.

For the member countries, the CCT meant both the loss of **customs revenue**, which has become a resource of the Community budget [see section 5.4.2], and the loss of the possibility of carrying out independent customs and trade policies. As of 1968, **the Member States are not entitled to unilaterally carry out customs policy**. No member country can unilaterally decide on or negotiate tariff matters. All changes to the CCT are decided by the Council following negotiation (if necessary) and proposal by the Commission. All bilateral (between the EU and non-member countries) and multilateral (inside the World Trade Organisation) negotiations are carried out by the Commission [see section 4.2.4].

6.1.6. What are the effects of the customs union?

The removal of customs duties and quantitative restrictions on imports and exports thanks to the customs union provided **formidable stimulus to intra-Community trade** and became the foundation for the common market and all the common policies related to it. The most meaningful outcome of the customs union is the lightening of the administrative burden of companies carrying out intra-Community sales and purchases and, therefore, the encouragement of intra-Community transactions. Such exceptional trade growth was a key factor to economic development and the raising of the standard of living in all member countries of the original

EEC. The stimulating effect of the wider market created a feeling of business confidence, which resulted in investment growth.

The realisation of the customs union has also had important effects for the consumers of the member countries. It **contributed to their material wellbeing**, through a remarkable increase of better quality goods at prices lower than before tariff dismantling. Tangible manifestations of the customs union are the products from all over the continent, which are available at affordable prices in local stores in all the Member States. The customs union has also greatly facilitated the travel of the citizens from one country of the EC/EU to another. Hence, the welfare objective of European integration was well pursued through the customs union [see section 1.1].

At the same time, however, there has been a growing globalisation of illicit traffic in all areas, such as drugs, arms and human beings. From a customs viewpoint, this requires strengthened cooperation and **mutual assistance between the customs administrations** of Community countries and those of third countries, notably those of other European countries. A delicate balance needs to be struck by the customs' officers between ensuring minimum disruption to legitimate trade and free circulation of persons inside the customs union, and the need to detect and deter fraud and illegal activities related to it.

6.2. The common market stage

6.2.1. What is a common market?

The **common market** is a stage in the multinational integration process, which, in the words of a Court of Justice ruling, aims to remove all the barriers to intra-Community trade with a view to the merger of national markets into a **single market** giving rise to conditions as close as possible to a genuine **internal market**. In other words, the goal of the common market stage is the creation of an "internal market" which, according to Article 14 of the EC Treaty, should comprise "an area without internal frontiers in which the free movement of goods, persons, services and capital is ensured in accordance with the provisions of this Treaty".

The launch of the common market stage first required the **elimination of all import and export duties** existing between Member States before the foundation of the Community. We saw above how the Member States effectively removed the customs barriers even before expiration of the period laid down by the Treaty [see section 6.1.2] and how immediately after tariff dismantling, they began erecting other barriers between them [see section 6.1.3], in particular technical barriers which, in some cases, were even more difficult to overcome.

The halfway elimination of trade obstacles thanks to the customs union gave satisfactory but not optimal results for the economies of the original Member States. It thus revealed the necessity for the completion of the common market and for more common policies linked to it. In fact, the original Member States [see section 2.1] realised that, in order **to turn their customs union into a real internal market**, they would need to ensure not only the free movement of goods and services, but also the free movement of production factors, namely labour and capital. In order to obtain these fundamental freedoms of a common market [see section 6.2.2], the member states had to develop a great number of common policies, such as regional, social, environment and consumer protection, calling for further sharing of national sovereignties [see sections 1.3.4 and 6.2.8]. Several amendments of the EEC Treaty, through the Single European Act, were needed to bring about this evolution [see section 3.1.2].

6.2.2. What are the four freedoms of the common market?

The creation of a common market similar to an internal market implies not only the liberalisation of trade among the participating member states but also necessitates the **free movement of production factors**: labour, capital and services. It further entails the free establishment of persons and companies in all the territory of the member states, in order to exercise their professional or business activities.

Hence, in order to speak about a common market, we need to have between the constituent member states the existence of four **fundamental freedoms**: freedom of movement of goods, thanks to the elimination of all trade barriers; freedom of movement of salaried and non salaried workers, thanks to the elimination of all restrictions to their entrance and residence in other Member States; freedom of establishment of persons and companies in the territory of any Member State and of the provision of services by them in the host country; and freedom of capital movements for business or personal purposes. It appears that the **keyword of the common market is freedom**.

6.2.3. How was the free movement of goods achieved?

Tariff disarmament completed thanks to the customs union, in July 1968, had eliminated customs barriers to intra-Community trade [see section 6.1.2]. But there still remained technical obstacles to trade and the EEC Treaty had not fixed a timetable for their elimination. **Technical barriers to trade result from national regulations** obliging the producers of industrial products and foodstuffs to satisfy certain criteria or to meet certain standards and technical specifications. This legislation is necessary for various reasons: standardising industrial production, guaranteeing the safety of workers, protecting the health of consumers and preventing or reducing environmental pollution, etc. The problem for the common market was not the existence of national regulations, but the differences between them and also the fact that those regulations could be used to protect the national market from products from other Member States which were subject to different standards.

The removal of technical obstacles to trade in **industrial products** is normally based on Article 94 of the EC Treaty, which provides for the **approximation of** such **provisions** laid down by law, regulation or administrative action that directly affect the functioning of the common market. On this legal basis, the Commission has for many years been trying to align national regulations with Community standards agreed upon in Council directives. The approximation of standardisation regulations leads to results which are **very useful for economic integration**. Indeed, once the standards are the same in all member countries, type approval of a product granted in any member country is recognised by all the others and can be sold in their markets. The manufacturers need only guarantee that all examples of a product conform to the approved prototype and hence to the specifications of the relevant harmonisation directive. But, the harmonisation of legislations is also very useful for consumers, since it guarantees them the quality and safety of products circulating in the large market.

The approximation of regulations is not, however, as easy as it seems at first sight. As technical regulations relate to production systems and consequently investments already made, and as their harmonisation sometimes entails the need for industrialists in some Member States to change their production systems by means of new investment expenditure, the removal of technical obstacles to trade used to be the subject of interminable discussions. Each member country tried to persuade its partners that its own technical regulations were the best and should be adopted by the Community.

Therefore, the approximation of regulations has been simplified. In cases where full harmonisation of technical standards cannot be applied, because divergences are too great between the essential aims of different national laws, legislative harmonisation is confined to the adoption of the **essential safety requirements** (or other requirements in the general interest) with which products must conform, in order to enjoy free movement throughout the EU. A **single "CE" marking** is used in order to facilitate controls on the Community market by inspectors and to clarify the obligations of economic operators in respect of marking under the various Community regulations. Consumers who see the "CE" (Communitas Europaea) marking on a product thus have an indication (not necessarily the proof) that it has been manufactured in conformity with Community standards.

6.2.4. How was the free movement of persons achieved?

One of the first priorities of the original European Economic Community was the free movement of the labour force. Under Article 39 of the EC Treaty (Art. 48 EEC), freedom of movement of workers entails the right, subject to limitations justified on grounds of public policy, public security or public health to accept offers of employment actually made, **to move freely** within the territory of Member States for this purpose, **to stay** in a Member State for the purpose of employment and **to remain** in the territory of that Member State after having been employed in it. The Community legislation that materialised those principles was completed in 1968 and, thus, freedom of movement of workers was achieved, from the legal point of view, at the same time as the customs union for products [see section 6.1.2]. The worker and his or her family members who have resided in a host Member State during a continuous period of five years have a right of permanent residence in that State. The members of the family enjoy the right of residence even after the worker's death.

Nowadays, free movement is not restricted to workers. Article 18 of the EC Treaty gives every **citizen of the Union the right to move and reside freely** within the territory of the Member States.

A citizen of the European Union who no longer enjoys a right of residence as a migrant worker in the host Member State can, as a citizen of the Union, enjoy a right of residence there by direct application of Article 18(1) EC. The same right is enjoyed by his spouse, their descendants under the age of 21 and their dependent relatives in the ascending line. This right contributes to a concrete and practical expression of European citizenship. For periods of residence of longer than three months, Member States may only require Union citizens to register with the competent authorities in the place of residence.

Adequate protection by European **provisions in the field of social security** is necessary for the effective use of the right of the citizens of one Member State to stay and work in another State of the Union. Without such protection, persons moving across borders to work or to look for a job, would risk losing all or part of their rights acquired or in the process of being acquired under national legislation (concerning, for example pensions, health insurance, unemployment benefits or family benefits). Therefore, on the basis of Article 42 of the EC Treaty many measures have been adopted for the adequate social protection of workers residing in partner countries. Concerning health insurance in particular, any insured person staying temporarily, for tourist or employment purposes, in a Member State other than the one in which he or she is insured may be admitted to hospital or receive refunds in respect of urgent medical care in the host State on presentation of the **European health insurance card**.

The transformation of the economic migratory movements of the post-war period into free movement of workers is one of the great achievements of European integration. The freedom of movement of salaried and non-salaried workers allows EU citizens to seek, within the Union, **better living and working conditions** than are available to them in their region of origin. It therefore boosts greatly the chances of improving the standards of living of the individual. At the same time, freedom of movement reduces social pressure in the poorest regions of the European Union and allows the living conditions of those remaining to improve.

6.2.5. How was the freedom of establishment of persons and companies achieved?

Freedom of establishment includes the right to take up and pursue **activities as self-employed persons and to set up and manage undertakings**, in particular companies established under the conditions laid down for its own nationals by the law of the country where such establishment is effected. According to Article 43 of the EC Treaty, the freedom of establishment of companies extends to what is known as freedom of secondary establishment, i.e. the setting up of agencies, branches or subsidiaries. This article has direct effect (does not need special Community legislation in order to be applied) and, therefore, any individual may, on its basis demand directly the same treatment as is applied to nationals.

Whereas freedom to provide services chiefly concerns the pursuit of an economic activity by a person in another Member State without having the principal or secondary place of business in that State, **right of establishment entails permanent installation** in another Member State in order to pursue an economic activity in that State. Therefore, the right for citizens of EU Member States to work or pursue activities as self-employed persons in the Member States means the **right to enter and to reside** in the member country in which they wish to work or pursue those activities. This right is extended to their spouses, children and other members of their families, including the registered partner if the legislation of the host Member State treats registered partnership as equivalent to marriage.

Obvious discriminatory practices in the pursuit of an economic activity in other Member States were removed early enough. There remained, however, other obstacles to the freedom of establishment, i.e. the numerous requirements of the Member States with regard to the training of employed and self-employed persons, and the detailed arrangements for pursuing industrial and commercial activities. These requirements could impede the free establishment, if they differed from country to country and obliged the interested person to take a new examination for the recognition of his or her professional competence. Therefore, the Community has adopted a **general system for the recognition of higher-education diplomas** awarded on completion of professional education and training of at least three years' duration. A similar system relates to diplomas and certificates awarded on completion of **professional education and training of fewer than three years** of higher education or not covered by higher education. A simple mechanism also exists for **recognising qualifications for professional activities** outside the scope of the general systems above, notably in the distributive trade and craft sectors. These systems are based on the principle of the equivalence of qualifications obtained in various Member States. With these general systems, any EU national has the right to have vocational qualifications obtained in another Member State recognised in respect of any host Member State which regulates any activity whatsoever in its territory.

6.2.6. How was the free provision of services achieved?

Article 49 (TEC) declares that **restrictions on freedom to provide services within the Community shall be abolished** in respect of nationals of Member States who are established in a State of the Community other than that of the person for whom the services are intended. Any discrimination concerning the provision of services on the basis of nationality is prohibited directly by this Article (without the need of specific Community legislation).

The person providing a service may, in order to do so, temporarily pursue his or her activity in the State where the service is provided, under the same conditions as are imposed by that State on its own nationals. There is nothing, moreover, to preclude an activity for the provision of services from being of a magnitude such as to necessitate the acquisition of real estate in the country of provision of services. However, to constitute a provision of services rather than a permanent establishment, the person providing the service **must remain established in his own country and his services must cross borders**. It appears that the freedom of establishment and the freedom to provide services cannot be clearly distinguished in all situations and that they often go together, since a person or company establishes himself or herself in another Member State in order to provide services in that state. This is why the two freedoms are usually considered as **one: the freedom of establishment and provision of services**.

Services represent almost 60% of the value added of the Community economy and cover a vast spread of economic activities, from banks and insurance to transport and tourism, not to mention data processing and management consultancy. They therefore play an increasingly large part in the economy and employment and are a lynchpin for smooth operation of the EU's internal market. Their liberalisation is based on **the principle of mutual recognition**, according to which, if a service is lawfully authorised in one Member State it must be open to users in the other Member States without having to comply with every detail of the legislation of the host country, except those concerning consumer protection. Control has to be exercised by the Government in the territory of which the company providing the services is established.

Financial services - banks, insurance companies and stock exchanges - which are closely monitored by the official authorities, are particularly important, as they constitute a vast market and are indispensable for the proper functioning of the other economic sectors. The freedoms of establishment and provision of services in the common market required that those services be liberalised from the protectionist measures applied by most Member States. This liberalisation, however, should satisfy the need to maintain very stringent criteria for control and financial security.

Under these conditions, all restrictions on freedom of establishment and freedom to provide services in respect of self-employed activities of **banks and other financial institutions** have been abolished since the 1970s. The laws, regulations and administrative provisions of the Member States relating to the taking up and pursuit of the business of credit institutions have been coordinated within a single regulatory framework. The right of access is based on the mutual recognition of supervision systems, i.e. application of the principle of supervision of a credit institution by the Member State in which it has its head office, and the issue of a "**single bank licence**" which is valid throughout the Community. The single licence authorises a bank established in a Member State to open branches without any other formalities or to propose its services in the partner countries.

A **single authorisation system enables an insurance company** with its registered office in a Community Member State to open branches and operate services in all the Member States without the need for authorisation procedures in each country. This system is designed to ensure the free movement of insurance products within the Community and give European citizens the opportunity to take out insurance with any Community insurer, thus finding the coverage best suited to their needs at the lowest cost, while enjoying an adequate level of protection.

The conditions for the admission of securities to official **stock exchange** listing have also been coordinated in order to form the single market in securities. An investment firm in any Member State can carry out its activities anywhere in the European Union on the basis of a single authorisation (called a "European passport) issued by the Member State of origin. However, investment services in the securities field are monitored throughout the EU financial area by the Directive on markets in financial instruments, which ensures that investors enjoy a high level of protection when employing investment firms, wherever they are located in the EU.

6.2.7. How was the freedom of capital movements achieved?

The liberalisation of payment transactions is a vital **complement to the free movement of goods, persons and services**. Borrowers - individuals and companies - must be able to obtain capital where it is cheapest and best tailored to their needs, while investors and suppliers of capital must be able to offer their resources on the market where there is the greatest interest. Article 56 (TEC) declares, in fact, that all restrictions on the movement of capital between Member States and between Member States and third countries are prohibited. However, Article 58 (TEC) authorises Member States to take all requisite measures to prevent infringements of national law and regulations, in particular in the field of taxation and the prudential supervision of financial institutions.

On the basis of these provisions and of those liberalising banking, stock-exchange and insurance services [see section 6.2.6], the Community financial market has been completely liberalised since January 1, 1993. **European businesses and individuals have access to the full range of options** available in the Member States as regards banking services, mortgage loans, securities and insurance. They are able to choose what is best suited to their specific needs or requirements for their daily lives and for their professional activities in the large market. The Member States must, however, dissuade the exploitation of the financial market for illegal purposes, notably **laundering money generated by criminal activities**. The Community legislation obliges them to take measures such as identification of customers and economic beneficiaries, the conservation of supporting documents and registrations of the transactions, the informing of the relevant authorities of suspected laundering operations and the determination of applicable sanctions.

6.2.8. What are the effects of the common market?

The **achievement of a single market was a great step forward** in the process of European integration. Free movement reduces the manufacturing and transport costs of goods, facilitates exports and permits the realisation of important economies. The reduction of administrative and financial costs of intra-Community trade and the realisation of economies of scale tend to liberate the dynamism and the creativity of European businesses and to give them a solid base from which to tackle international competitiveness. In a global economy characterised by fierce competition, particularly between multinational companies, the economies and the companies of small and medium European countries would certainly be much worse off than they are today, if it was not for the large internal market that serves as a safe haven and springboard for external markets.

The implementation of the fundamental freedoms of the common market allows the **production factors of work and capital to operate without hindrance**. Businesses can manufacture and sell their products in accordance with a system of free competition in the Member State in which conditions are most advantageous to them. They can set themselves up wherever they wish in the common market and can call on a multitude of services and sources of capital, which exist in all the Member States. The liberalisation of capital movements contributes to a better allocation of resources within the Union. In banking and insurance sectors, where obstacles to cross-border trade were particularly pronounced, the increase in cross-border competition is reflected in a growing number of branches and outlets in all Member States of the Union.

The common market has also boosted the welfare of the citizens of the Member States. European consumers, previously confined to their respective national markets, now enjoy a huge choice of high quality goods and services at prices dictated by free competition. The free movement of workers, freedom to provide services and freedom of establishment for self-employed persons constitute **fundamental rights**, allowing the citizens of the Community to pursue an occupation in any Member State. The citizen of a Member State, be he or she worker, businessman or tourist, can no longer be regarded as an alien in another Member State, but as an EU citizen, and no discrimination against him or her is permitted.

The completion of the single market has furthermore speeded up the process of European integration. Indeed, the "acquis communautaire" on the single market had undeniable **spillover effects on practically all common policies** [see section 1.3.4]. It prompted a high degree of fiscal harmonisation, thereby removing fiscal frontiers. It created a need for strengthened economic and social cohesion and therefore prompted a major step forward for the Community's regional and social policies. It spurred progress on opening up European markets in electricity and gas, transport and telecommunications. It reinforced the legal foundations of consumer and environmental protection policies and those of research and development policies. Lastly and perhaps most importantly, consolidation of the single market was the driving force behind the

Maastricht agreements, designed to build economic and monetary union [see sections 3.2.1 and 6.3]. On the one hand, the single market provides underlying economic support for monetary union and the euro provides added value and efficiency to the single market.

All this **does not mean that all is well in the best possible single market**. There still is a need to make it work efficiently. This implies, in particular, adequate implementation of the measures taken for the completion of the internal market in every Member State, effective opening-up of public contracts, further mutual recognition of standards, more transparent rules for the internal market and simplification of the taxation systems. These requirements for the proper functioning of the common market are not met uniformly and constantly in all Member States. Hence, the common market is not yet a completely integrated internal market and this fact handicaps European companies competing in the global market with companies which have as a base a large internal market.

Moreover, although the common market provides a basis for common policies, it cannot by itself solve the structural problems weighing on European economies. Strong common economic, industrial and research policies are needed to hasten the modernisation of European economies and to enhance the competitiveness of European companies in the global market. These policies can and should also boost employment, while safeguarding the European social model. It is an illusion to think that European citizens may be satisfied with a common market that promotes the interests of businesses and not their own interests as workers and consumers. They rightly see the common market not as an end in itself but as a means to their own welfare [see section 2.1.1]. If it is not successful to this end, the common market is an incomplete tool and European leaders should perfect it.

6.3. The economic and monetary union stage

Economic and monetary union (EMU) is **an advanced stage of multinational integration** involving a common monetary policy and closely coordinated economic policies of the member states. EMU has to be based on a common market in goods and services but is itself necessary for the proper functioning of the common market, as exchange rate variations between Member States' currencies hinder trade and investments. If economic conditions in the common market are to resemble those in an internal market, it is first and foremost necessary to eliminate exchange rate adjustments, which disrupt trade and investment by altering in an unpredictable way their profitability.

6.3.1. Why did the majority of EU States want to move to the stage of economic and monetary union?

During the stage of the customs union, exchange rate variations are still possible and, to a certain extent, desirable, because the member states conserve the autonomy of their economic policies and can, by means of those variations, adjust their economies to the new conditions of competition prevailing between themselves and between themselves and the rest of the world. The stage of the **common market, however, generates situations that are unstable**, and in the long term intolerable, for member states' economic policies. Those policies are no longer sufficient for regulating short-term economic situations because, firstly, some of their elements are found abroad (in other Member States and in the global market) and, secondly, some economic policy instruments are already beyond the control of the national authorities, including customs duties, import restrictions and export incentives.

In reality, the interdependence of the economies of members of a common market accelerates the **transmission of cyclical fluctuations** and of the effects of measures intended to deal with them. Attainment of the economic objectives of a member state depends to a large extent on economic conditions in the other member states. An unfavourable economic situation in one member state leads to a reduction in its imports from the other members of the common market, which are affected in turn. On the other hand, a favourable economic situation in one member country has positive effects on the economies of the others and feedback effects on the former. If there were no coordination of economic policies, the differences in economic development - which would take the form of high interest rates in some member states and low rates in others and, conversely, of low exchange rates in the former and high exchange rates in the latter - could result in undesirable capital movements, that is to say from the poorest to the richest countries [see section 6.2.7]. Hence, if the common market were divided into autonomous markets as a result of divergent economic policies followed by the member states, the anticipated advantages, in particular economic growth and economic stability, would be greatly reduced.

Negative effects can also ensue from **divergences in national short-term economic policies**. If, for example, a member state wished to pursue a deflationary policy by raising interest rates, whilst another member state followed an expansionist policy with low interest rates, capital would emigrate, for short-term investments, from the second country to the first and prevent the attainment of the objectives of both. Even if they pursued the same objectives but by different means, two member states of a common market without a single currency could bring about undesirable movements of capital [see section 6.2.7]. If, for example, in order to pursue a deflationary policy, a state imposed quantitative restrictions on credit, whilst another raised interest rates, capital from the first might go to short-term investment in the second, causing balance of payments problems in the first and inflationary pressures in the second.

Moreover, a common market influences the monetary conditions of the member states and perturbs national monetary policies. The **exchange rate variations become more and more inconvenient** for the partners. While equal conditions of competition should prevail in a common market, the devaluation of the currency of a Member State could provide a competitive advantage to its industries, whereas the revaluation of the currency of another Member State could handicap its exports. In fact, **the devaluation** of the currency of a country which is a member of a common market could have an equivalent effect to imposing customs tariffs on all imported products and subsidising that country's exports. Conversely, **the revaluation** of a member country's currency would mean restricting its exports and encouraging its imports, factors which could get in the way of business expansion in countries with strong currencies.

Currency fluctuations can penalise both investors who have financed their **foreign investments** by exporting capital from their countries and those who have had recourse to the resources of the host country. In the first case, devaluation of the currency of the country in which the investment took place or revaluation of the currency of the investor's country erodes the repatriated capital and profits. In the second case, devaluation in the investor's country or revaluation in the host country means higher amortisation and therefore a greater investment cost than expected. These risks could hinder businesses from investing in partner countries or from borrowing in them capital needed for their investments. Exchange risks, thus, would limit interpenetration of financial markets [see sections 6.2.6 and 6.2.7] and therefore economic growth in a single market without a single currency.

For all these reasons, the majority of the Member States felt that the semi-integration or imperfect integration, which characterises a common market, would lead to a **dwindling of the independence of national economic policies.** They understood that, after the completion of the single market in 1992, their economies could not be managed effectively by national authorities, i.e. the appropriate ministries and national central banks. They believed that the loss of autonomy of their national economic and monetary policies inside the single market should be counterbalanced by the establishment of a single monetary policy and of a common economic policy. Hence, they sensed the need to pass to the next stage of multinational integration, which is that of economic and monetary union.

6.3.2. What does the economic and monetary union entail?

In order to establish a monetary union, the member states of a common market must agree the full and **irreversible conversion of their currencies** at fixed parities or, better, **adopt a single currency**. In either case, they would need to establish a monetary union within which transaction costs (the costs of foreign-exchange transactions or the costs of exchange rate cover) would disappear altogether. The second possibility, however, which was rightly preferred by the EU, has some additional advantages. The single currency permits a genuine comparison of prices of goods and services within the single market. It is one of the main exchange and reserve currencies in the world and it allows Europeans to pay for their imports from third countries in their own currency.

In other words, **the single currency is a necessary attribute of a genuine single market.** This is the reason why, in view of the completion of the single market, the Member States of the Community decided, in December 1991, in Maastricht [see section 3.2.1] to pursue the path of economic and monetary union. By greatly facilitating the functioning of the single market, the single currency should provide a stable macroeconomic environment, which would be of considerable benefit to businesses. Under ceteris paribus conditions, this environment should foster trade, improve the allocation of resources, encourage savings, enhance growth and in the end create more employment.

Certainly, all these benefits would be derived from the economic and monetary union under **certain conditions**. The monetary union should encompass only countries well managed economically; hence the **need for an economic union**, within which member states would have undertaken to scrupulously observe certain criteria ensuring monetary stability, price stability, sound public finances and, thus, sustainable growth. The observance of these criteria would be based on two foundations: an independent central bank, which would determine the union's monetary policy; and a centre for the coordination of economic policies, responsible for defining the broad guidelines of economic policy and having the means at its disposal to apply pressure on participating countries to meet their commitments [see section 6.3.6]. A new Treaty, the Treaty on the European Community was signed in Maastricht [see section 3.2.1], in order to establish these criteria and to place the foundations of this new stage of European integration.

6.3.3. Why did some members of the EC/EU opt out of the single currency?

The establishment of an **EMU certainly means the loss of monetary sovereignty** of the countries participating in the final stage of the EMU [see section 6.3.4] and even some loss of their economic independence, notably because the exchange rate instrument cannot be used anymore by one of these countries experiencing particular difficulties. Countries that were always repulsed by the sharing of sovereignties principle entailed in the multinational integration process [see section 1.2.1] declined this major conferral of competences to supranational institutions [see section 6.3.6]. They certainly had many arguments for their position, the main thrust of which was that a single currency was a novel experiment that could harm their economies. They could postpone their participation until some conditions were met and until the experiment had proved its soundness.

Although the change-over to the single currency was an unmitigated success and has not brought major difficulties to the economies of the twelve countries which have adopted it [see section 6.3.9], it is still too early to conclude that these economies are better off than those of the countries, which have kept their national currencies. Therefore, the latter can still wait until the euro proves that it has more advantages than disadvantages for the countries, which have adopted it.

The only sure fact to date is that, in order to create the conditions of a single market, the partners have already adopted a great number of common policies and, thus, have lost a good deal of the possibility of autonomous management of their economies [see section 6.3.1]. Hence, the independence of economic and monetary policies in a common market is problematical, not to say unfeasible. This loss of national autonomy in the economic field can only be compensated by the **development of collective disciplines**. The countries which shy away from shared sovereignties rightly fear that participation in the euro zone would engage them in an "ever closer union" with their partners. They would thus have to participate in the policies and share the gains and losses of the common enterprise with their partners, whereas they believe that they can fare better with the small independence of action that they still have.

6.3.4. How was the economic and monetary union prepared?

The Treaty of Rome did not provide for the monetary organisation of the Community because that Treaty aimed at the realisation of the first two stages of European integration the customs union and the common market [see section 3.1.2]. Moreover, at the time of drafting the EEC Treaty an international monetary organisation existed, namely the Bretton Woods system, which ensured the convertibility of all the currencies of the Western World at fixed parities. This system warranted monetary stability, which is indispensable in a common market.

It was just at the time when the Bretton Woods system collapsed, **in early 1971**, that the Member States of the Community **began their effort to organise their monetary affairs** in an economic and monetary union. Acting on a proposal from the Commission based on the "Werner Report", the Council and the Representatives of the Governments of the original six Member States [see section 2.2.2] expressed their political will to establish economic and monetary union in accordance with a phased plan beginning retroactively on 1 January 1971. At the conclusion of that process the Community was to have constituted a single currency area within the international system.

With hindsight, that initial effort looks like a headlong rush without sound foundations, as it was not based on a real common market, which was completed only in 1992 [see section 6.2.3]. However, that initial effort enabled the Members States to acquire precious experience and devise instruments and mechanisms that were, in 1979, transferred to the European Monetary System (which tried with variable success to stabilise the exchange rates of the common market countries), have been improved over time and were used for the second effort at establishing an economic and monetary union in the 1990s. This second effort had a better foothold than the first. The common market stage had been completed, the Member States had developed closer links through common policies and had engaged themselves in the Maastricht Treaty to advance to the stage of economic and monetary union.

The 1971 experience served the EU to prepare successfully the changeover to the single currency. Although economic and monetary union was envisaged as a single process, there were, in fact, **three stages involved**. The **first stage**, marking the beginning of the whole process, came about with the complete liberalisation of capital movements in July 1990 [see section 6.2.7]. The central objectives of this phase were greater convergence of economic policies and closer cooperation between central banks, incorporating greater consistency between monetary practices in the framework of the European Monetary System.

The **second stage** of economic and monetary union began on 1st January 1994 and ended on 31 December 1998. During that stage, the Treaty on European Union compelled each Member State to endeavour to avoid excessive public deficits and initiate steps leading to independence of its central bank, so that the future monetary union encompassed only countries which were well managed economically. A Council Regulation laid down detailed rules and definitions for the application of the **excessive deficit procedure (EDP)**, including the definition of public debt.

In **preparation for the move to the third stage**, the Treaty [see section 3.2.1] required a high degree of convergence assessed by reference to **four specific criteria**: (a) a rate of inflation which is close to that of the three best performing Member States in terms of price stability; (b) a government budgetary position without a deficit that is excessive, meaning a government deficit not exceeding 3% of GNP and total government debt not greater than 60% of GNP (subject to an appraisement by the Council deciding by qualified majority); (c) the durability of convergence achieved by the Member State being reflected in the long-term interest rate levels; and (d) the observance of the normal fluctuation margins provided for by the Exchange Rate Mechanism of the European Monetary System, for at least two years (Art. 121 TEC and Protocol on the excessive deficit procedure).

6.3.5. How was the change-over to the single currency achieved?

Following the procedure and the timetable set out in the EC Treaty, the Council, meeting at the level of Heads of State or Government on 3 May 1998, decided that 11 Member States **satisfied the necessary conditions for the adoption of the single currency** on 1 January 1999: Belgium, Germany, Spain, France, Ireland, Italy, Luxembourg, the Netherlands, Austria, Portugal and Finland. In July 2000, the Council agreed that Greece also fulfilled the convergence criteria and could therefore adopt the single currency. The Council had previously stated that Sweden did not at that stage fulfil the necessary conditions for the adoption of the single currency, because it did not participate in the mechanism of the European Monetary System. It did not examine whether the United Kingdom and Denmark fulfilled the conditions, because, in accordance with the relevant Treaty provisions, the United Kingdom notified the Council that it did not intend to move to the third stage of EMU on 1 January 1999 and Denmark notified the Council that it would not participate in the third stage of EMU [see section 6.3.3]. Member States benefiting from an "opt-out" and those which do not meet the criteria from the outset participate nevertheless in all the procedures (multilateral surveillance, excessive deficit...) designed to facilitate their future participation.

Stage three of EMU began on 1 January 1999 with the irrevocable fixing of conversion rates between the currencies of the participating countries and against the euro. The ecu was replaced by the euro, and this became a currency in its own right, the currency of those Member States which participate fully in the single monetary policy (Art. 123 TEC). From that date, monetary policy and the foreign exchange rate policy have been conducted in euros, the use of the euro has been encouraged in foreign exchange markets and new tradeable public debt had to be issued in euros by the participating Member States. The participating Member States have a single monetary policy and a single currency - the euro.

At 00.00 on 1 January 2002, **the national currencies of the twelve Euro-zone States ceased to exist**. After a short period of dual circulation, during which the old notes and coins were exchanged for the new ones, old banknotes can be exchanged for a period of ten years only at central banks. The European institutions and the governments of the participating Member States had carefully planned and therefore succeeded the tremendous enterprise of the changeover to the euro.

Citizens and businesses were certainly faced with **formidable problems in adapting their habits to the new currency**. For the former the problems were mainly psychological. They had to forsake their sentimental attachment to a national currency, in some cases very prestigious, like the Deutsche Mark and in some cases very old, like the Greek Drachma born more than 26 centuries ago. Consumers had to familiarise themselves with the euro and make the necessary effort to construct for themselves a new scale of values. Traders had to display prices and give change in euros. Businesses had to adapt their equipment, prepare to use a new currency and make the most of the increased competition within the single market resulting from greater price transparency. Despite these difficulties and the Cassandras' catastrophic prophesies, the euro was circulated successfully, thanks to an exemplary planning and cooperation of national and European authorities.

What these authorities had not foreseen and hence neglected was the attempt by many providers of goods and services to profit from the rounding possibilities offered by the new currency. This uncontrolled profiteering has increased inflationary pressures in economies already depressed from the unstable international environment [see section 6.3.9]. Particularly vulnerable were the consumers of countries having currencies with many zeros, like Italy and Greece, who did not immediately perceive the price increases in euro. In the long term, however, it is probable that heightened competition will stabilise prices inside the single market.

6.3.6. How is the single currency governed?

Since 1 January 1999, the participating Member States have a single currency, the euro and hence a single monetary policy which is exercised by the **European Central Bank (ECB)**, which forms, together with the central banks of the Member States, the **European System of Central Banks (ESCB).** Neither the ECB nor national central banks may seek or take instructions from governments or Community institutions (Art. 108 TEC). The Executive Board of the ECB, consisting of the President of the ECB, the Vice-President and four other members, implements the ECB monetary policy and gives the necessary instructions to the national central banks. The Executive Board is appointed by decision taken by common accord of the governments of the Member States, which have adopted the single currency [see section 6.3.5].

All central banks, including those not participating in the single monetary policy, are members of the ESCB. The **primary objec-**

tive of the ESCB is to maintain price stability. In addition, the ESCB must support the general economic policies in the Community with a view to contributing to the achievement of the objectives of the common policies referred to in Article 2 (TEC). The **basic tasks to be carried out through the ESCB** are: to define and implement the monetary policy of the Community; to conduct foreign exchange operations consistent with the provisions of Article 111 (TEC); to hold and manage the official foreign reserves of the Member States; and to promote the smooth operation of payment systems (Art. 105 TEC). However, exchange policy with regard to the currencies of third countries (US dollar, Japanese yen, etc.) is determined by the Council after consultation of the ECB (Article 111 TEC).

The ECB has the **exclusive right to authorise the issue of euro bank notes** within the Community. The ECB and the national central banks may issue such notes. Member States may issue euro coins subject to approval by the ECB of the volume of the issue (Art. 106 TEC). The **ECB** can adopt regulations and take decisions necessary for carrying out the tasks entrusted to the ESCB (Art. 110 TEC). National authorities must consult the ECB regarding draft legislation within its field of competence. The ECB must be consulted on any proposed Community act and may submit opinions to Community institutions or to national authorities on matters within its field of competence (Art. 105 TEC). The countries of the euro zone have thus conferred practically all their sovereign rights in the monetary field to common institutions [see section 3.3.2].

6.3.7. What is the stability and growth pact?

The move to the third stage of economic and monetary union has brought the economies of the Member States adopting the euro closer together. They share a single monetary policy and a single exchange rate. Economic policies and wage determination, however, remain a national responsibility, subject to the provisions of Article 104 (TEC). Since national economic developments have an impact on inflation prospects in the euro zone, they influence monetary conditions in that zone. It is for this reason that the management of the single currency requires closer Community surveillance and coordination of economic policies among euro zone Member States.

The Amsterdam European Council of 16 and 17 June 1997 therefore adopted a Resolution laying down the firm commitments of the Member States, the Commission and the Council regarding the implementation of the **Stability and Growth Pact**. In this Pact Member States are committed to: respecting the medium term budgetary objective of "close to balance or in surplus" set out in their stability or convergence programmes; correcting excessive deficits as quickly as possible after their emergence; making public, on their own initiative, recommendations made in accordance with Article 104 (TEC); and not seeking an exemption from the excessive deficit procedure unless they are in severe recession characterised by a fall in real GDP of at least 0,75%.

The Stability and Growth Pact asserts that Member States remain responsible for their national budgetary policies. It provides, however, both for **prevention and deterrence of excessive deficits** through two Regulations [see section 5.3.1]. The Regulation on the strengthening of the surveillance of budgetary positions requires Member States to submit stability programmes (or convergence programmes in the case of the countries not participating in the single currency) presenting the medium-term objective of a government budgetary position that is close to balance or surplus. The purpose of the second Regulation is to speed up and clarify the implementation of the excessive deficit procedure, in particular as regards the sanctions to be imposed on Member States which fail to take appropriate measures to correct an excessive deficit. Therefore, Member States are required to compile and transmit to the Commission data on their quarterly government debt.

European economies suffered dearly from the 11 September 2001 terrorist attacks on the United States, the Iraq invasion and occupation, the rising price of oil and the hindrance of European exports from the fall of the value of the dollar in relation to the euro. As a result of these external and unpredictable circumstances, **most economies of the euro zone were hit by stagnation and rising levels of unemployment**. In these circumstances, the Stability and Growth Pact, agreed in a state of euphoria, began looking like a straitjacket to some countries among the most important of the Eurozone. Since the Community always proceeds by trial and error, it seems likely that the Stability and Growth Pact will be adapted to the new circumstances without; however, abandoning the objective of the convergence of the Member States' economic policies [see section 6.3.10].

6.3.8. How is the objective of economic convergence pursued?

Since national economic developments have an impact on inflation prospects in the euro zone, they influence monetary conditions in that zone. It is for this reason that the single currency requires closer Community surveillance and coordination of economic policies among euro zone Member States. In order to ensure further convergence and the smooth functioning of the single market, non-participating Member States are included in the coordination of economic policies.

On the basis of the Treaty and specially agreed instruments, economic policy coordination concentrates on those national policies which have the potential to influence monetary and financial conditions throughout the euro area, the exchange rate of the euro, the smooth functioning of the single market as well as investment, employment and growth conditions in the Community. Thus, **economic policy coordination includes the close monitoring of:** macroeconomic developments; exchange rate developments of the euro and other EU currencies; budgetary positions and policies in accordance with the Treaty and the Stability and Growth Pact [see section 6.3.7]; nominal and real wage developments; and national employment action plans (NAPs), dealing in particular with active labour market policy.

Since the second stage of EMU, i.e. since 1 January 1994, national economic policies are coordinated at Community level with a view to Member States attaining progressive convergence of economic performance. To this effect the **Economic and Financial Affairs Council (ECOFIN)**, acting by a qualified majority on a recommendation from the Commission, formulates, each year in the spring, a draft for the **broad economic policy guidelines (BEPGs)** of the Member States and of the Community. On this basis, the Commission recommends and the Council, acting on a qualified majority endorses the BEPGs, which lay down the common objectives in terms of inflation, public finance, exchange rate stability and employment (Art. 99 TEC). The BEPGs are at the centre of economic policy coordination in the European Union.

The Council, on the basis of reports submitted by the Commission, monitors economic developments in each of the Member States and in the Community as well as the consistency of economic policies with the broad guidelines (Art 121 TEC). This **multilateral monitoring** is based on convergence programmes presented by each Member State which specifically aim at addressing the main sources of difficulty in terms of convergence (Art. 99,3 TEC). It also involves a review of budgetary policies, with particular reference to the size and financing of deficits, if possible prior to the drafting of national budgets. Multilateral monitoring aims at obtaining from the Member States reciprocal engagements for an autonomous coordination of their policies. Clearly, the Member States - and particularly those participating in the euro zone - share their competences in the economic field with the common institutions [see section 3.3.2].

6.3.9. What are the effects of economic and monetary union?

As happened with the first attempt at establishing an economic and monetary union in Europe, in 1971 [see section 6.3.4], the launch of the euro coincided with a **highly adverse international economic and monetary situation**: the terrorist attacks in New York and Madrid, the sizeable devaluation of the dollar, wars in Afghanistan and Iraq on Europe' doorstep and high energy prices, probably related to these wars. In this global situation, the economies of the euro zone have run into unexpected difficulties, largely due to outside factors: the strong competition in world markets from companies working with undervalued currencies; the equally strong competition from countries practicing social dumping, i.e. countries with no social protection and therefore extremely cheap labour force; high prices of imported oil; and last but not least, the precarious situation in the Middle East. In this adverse global situation, the euro has shielded the economies of the euro zone from competitive devaluations, galloping inflation and an increase in the prices of imports, more than 60% of which come from other euro countries. It is highly probable that if European economies had not the shield of the euro, they would have been in a much worse situation than the one in which they found themselves when the euro became the strongest currency in the world.

In practical terms, the second effort at creating a European economic and monetary union was **an unquestionable success**, particularly in view of the great challenge of the changeover to the single currency. Not only was the physical introduction of the euro a historic event, it also represented an unprecedented strategic, logistical and practical challenge. From one day to the next, several million coin-operated machines and several hundred thousand automatic cash dispensers (ATMs) had to be recalibrated. Some 15 billion euro banknotes and 50 billion euro coins replaced, in the space of a few weeks, a broadly equivalent quantity of national notes and coins in twelve countries with a combined population of some three hundred million.

The most direct "static gain" of the EMU is the **ending, within the unified market, of all transaction costs** inherent in the use of several currencies, costs representing between 0.3 and 0.4% of the GDP of the Union. Travellers, who previously lost important amounts in the exchange of their currency for those of the countries they visited, should particularly welcome these gains. "Dynamic gains", which cannot be measured directly, could take two forms: those resulting from heightened productivity and those generated by the elimination of the uncertainties concerning the long-term evolution of exchange rates.

Moreover, in spite of the great advance of multinational integration brought about by the EMU, national sovereignties have not suffered unduly. The Member States, which have moved to the third stage of EMU, have undoubtedly **lost the autonomy of their monetary policy**, since they are no longer at liberty to use the two main levers of this policy - the exchange rates and the interest rates (a freedom which they had already lost to a large extent, due to the interdependence of the European economies) [see section 6.3.1]. At the same time, however, they lost responsibility for the parity of their currency and the equilibrium of their balance of payments, while enjoying shared responsibility for the parity of the euro against the currencies of third countries and the equilibrium of the collective balance of payments of the euro-zone countries. However, balance of current payments constraints exist for the zone as a whole. Therein lies the importance of the close coordination of economic policies [see section 6.3.10].

In the global context, the euro allows a better balance of the international monetary system, dominated for half a century by the dollar, which serves as a reference currency for almost 60% of world trade, whereas American exports represent around 12% of world exports. Its economic and commercial weight (16% of world exports) entitles the Union to play an important role in the necessary **review of the international monetary and financial system**. This review should focus on methods of crisis prevention and management, improved governance of the international monetary and financial system, development assistance and debt relief for developing countries.

6.3.10. How can the economic and monetary union be further consolidated?

As a matter of fact, the economic and monetary union is still in a trial phase. It has not consolidated itself. It suffers, in particular, from disequilibrium between its strong monetary wing and its feeble economic one. The euro area is a monetary union working under a single monetary policy and **coordinated but decentralised economic policies**. While monetary policy management is the exclusive responsibility of the European Central Bank [see section 6.3.6], economic and budgetary policies are a national prerogative [see section 6.3.8]. However, in an integrated monetary and economic zone, overspending and deficient restraint of inflation rates in some countries inflict a collective cost borne by all the countries sharing the same currency. There is a need, therefore, to reinforce existing economic, in particular fiscal, policy coordination mechanisms within the euro area and improve monitoring and evaluation of euro-area economic trends, including inflation, wage increases, investments and euro exchange rates.

As for other common policies, it is essential to have at the heart of the system **a body responsible for stating the general interest** and for bolstering the credibility and the cohesiveness of the system in the face of threats to the whole euro zone. This role falls naturally upon the Commission, whose role should be strengthened [see section 5.2.3]. Thus, the instruments of economic policy coordination, particularly the major economic policy guidelines and the opinions on the stability and convergence programmes, should be drafted on the basis of proposals from the Commission, from which the Council could depart only by unanimity (not by qualified majority).

The **Stability and Growth Pact instrument is not a goal as such** but clarifies and confirms the preventive and meritorious objective of the provisions of the Treaty concerning surveillance and coordination of the Member States' economic policies [see section 6.3.8]. A revised stability and growth pact should aim at creating the conditions to foster employment and investment, while adhering to the medium-term objective of a budgetary position close-to-balance or in surplus. The strategy should be built upon further reductions of public debt, increases in employment rates and reforms of pension systems. Moreover, the EMU calls for stronger common structural and social policies. Otherwise the current structural imbalance between the Member States could worsen within the monetary union.

6.4. The political union stage

6.4.1. What is a political union?

Political union is the last stage of the multinational integration process. It involves **common home and judicial policies and a common foreign and security policy**. The stage of political union, however, requires the implementation by all the participating states of the common home and foreign policies agreed by the common institutions and the monitoring of this implementation by the common institutions [see section 1.3.1]. As long as these requirements are not met in the foreign and security sectors, political union, even though provided in a Treaty [see section 3.2], is deficient or inexistent. In its place there may only exist intergovernmental political cooperation, leaving practically all freedom of action to the participants - a freedom incompatible with the definition of a common policy [see section 1.2.1].

In fact, the guidelines for the common policies in this area have to be clearly set out in a treaty signed and ratified by all participating member states and the common policies that result from those guidelines have to be agreed by the common institutions according to the rules prescribed in this treaty. Such agreement presupposes that all member states participating at this stage have a common interest in a common policy worked out by the common institutions [see section 1.3.1]. Such common interest is difficult to be found in an area where national geopolitical interests have been built over the centuries. Hence, political integration cannot be built overnight. Time is needed to foster common political interests among formerly antagonistic nations and, therefore, to build common policies to pursue them. It ensues that the stage of political union is **the most difficult part of the multinational integration process**, because it requires recognition by all Member States of the fact that they have common interests in the fields of foreign and security policies [see section 1.3.3]. The problem is certainly complicated, since the transition to the stage of political union requires the unanimity of the Member States and some of them are clearly against the conferrals of power to supranational institutions that this union would entail [see section 2.1.2].

6.4.2. What do the European Treaties provide concerning the political union stage?

At the same time as they were preparing the economic and monetary union stage, at Maastricht in 1991, europhilic nations were also projecting their political union. They, of course, encountered the opposition of their eurosceptic partners [see sections 2.1.2 and 6.3.3]. The compromise solution that was found there and then was the division of the European Union into **two Treaties** (that of the European Community and that of the European Union) [see section 3.2.1] and into **three construction pillars**: the European Community (EC - the first and major pillar); common foreign and security policy (CFSP); and justice and home affairs (JHA).

The first and by far the more important Treaty (although coming second under the general heading of the Maastricht and now the Nice Treaties) and the first pillar or wing of the EC/EU edifice were to direct and regulate the first three stages of European integration: customs union, the common market and the projected economic and monetary union. The second Treaty and the second and third pillars were intended to prepare and manage the stage of political union. The European Community Treaty and hence the first pillar of the EC/EU provided for the governance of the first three stages of European integration by the existing common institutions using the well established Community decision-making procedure [see section 5.2.1]. The European Union Treaty, which was to guide and supervise the construction of the second and third pillars of the Union, prescribed for this construction the **intergovernmental cooperation method** [see section 1.2.1].

It was soon apparent that this method was leading nowhere towards the construction of the second and third pillars of the Union and, therefore, the progress of political integration. The disappointment was most felt in the area of the third pillar, where there were matters of common interest to be regulated urgently: the free circulation of citizens and residents of the Member States, a common immigration policy and a common protection of the external borders of the Union from all sorts of illegal trafficking. Concerning the first of these matters, europhilic nations had already taken the lead by signing, in June 1990, the **Schengen agreement** for the abolition of border checks between them. But, the need was felt by all Member States, first, to generalise the experience gained by the pioneers to all the partners and, second, to extend it to other matters of common interest. This need led to the revision of the European Union Treaty, at Amsterdam in 1997 [see section 3.2.2]. Most of the justice and home affairs pillar (notably questions relating to the free movement of persons, asylum, immigration, the crossing of external borders and judicial cooperation in civil matters) was placed under the Community orbit, where the efficacious Community decision-making procedurc is used [see section 5.2.1].

The **Constitutional Treaty** proposed to go a step further, by extending the community method to virtually all aspects of the field of justice and home affairs, thus abolishing the so-called third pillar of the Union. All measures would be adopted in the form of laws or framework laws through the normal legislative procedure, thus abolishing the current panoply of acts such as common positions and framework decisions [see section 3.3]. Common policies would be developed in the fields of border controls, visas, asylum and immigration (Art III-265).

The method of construction of the second pillar of the Union, that of the **common foreign and security policy** was not altered much by the Amsterdam and Nice Treaties on the European Union [see section 3.2.3] and, hence, this construction has progressed little, if at all [see sections 6.4.5 and 6.4.6]. It is no wonder, therefore, that the Member States of the Union were radically divided when their supposedly common foreign and security policy was tested for the first tome: the March 2003 war and occupation of Iraq under American aegis, without the consent of the Security Council of the United Nations. The **Constitutional Treaty** did very little to improve the method of construction of the second pillar of the Union [see section 3.3.5], which thus resembles an impressive edifice sheltering internal economic and other common policies, but an edifice without any door to the outside other than the small windows possibly opened by the foreign policies of the Member States, provided these are not contradictory.

6.4.3. What is included in judicial cooperation in civil matters?

The main objective in this area is legal certainty and equal access to justice for all EU citizens, implying easy identification of the competent jurisdiction, clear designation of the applicable law, availability of speedy and fair proceedings and effective enforcement procedures. Procedural rules should respond to broadly the same guarantees, ensuring that people will not be treated unevenly according to the jurisdiction dealing with their case. The principle of **mutual recognition of judicial decisions and judgments**, already implemented by several Community instruments, concerns notably general jurisdiction and special jurisdiction in matters relating to insurance, consumer contracts, individual contracts of employment and court settlements.

Concerning nationals of third countries, the abolition of internal border controls and the notion of a common external border [see section 6.2.4] reinforced the desirability for the Union to develop more common approaches and closer cooperation in the immigration policy area. In fact, the **abolition of checks at internal borders** of the Community is effective both for the citizens of the Member States and for third country nationals, once they have crossed the external frontiers of a Member State. This is why, the Member States must have common rules for the crossing of their external borders by foreigners and for the treatment of foreigners within their territory. This common need has led to the adoption of common policies in the fields of visas, immigration, the right of asylum, the status of refugees and extradition.

6.4.4. What is included in judicial cooperation in criminal matters?

Article 29 of the TEU declares that the Union's objective is to provide citizens with **a high level of safety** within an area of freedom, security and justice. This objective means that criminal behaviours need to be approached in the same way throughout the Union. In concrete terms, terrorism, corruption, traffic in human beings and organised crime should be the subject of minimum common rules relating to the constituent elements of criminal acts, and should be pursued with the same vigour wherever they take place.

Judicial cooperation in criminal matters includes: compatibility of rules applicable in the Member States; prevention of conflicts of jurisdiction between Member States; and the progressive establishment of common rules relating to the constituent elements of criminal acts and to penalties in the fields of organised crime, terrorism and illicit drug trafficking (Art. 31 TEU). **Police cooperation** is organised both directly between the administration of the Member States and through the **European Police Office (Europol)**, set up in 1995. Europol's remit includes the fight against terrorism, drug trafficking, forgery of money and means of payment, trade in human beings and the sexual exploitation of children.

6.4.5. What is meant by common foreign and security policy?

According to Article 2 of the Treaty on European Union [see section 3.2], the Union has set itself among its objectives: "to assert its identity on the international scene, in particular through the implementation of a common foreign and security policy including the progressive framing of a common defence policy, which might lead to a common defence". According to Article 11 of the TEU, the **objectives of CFSP** are: to safeguard the common values, fundamental interests, independence and integrity of the Union; to strengthen the security of the Union in all ways; to preserve peace and strengthen international security; to promote international co-operation; to develop and consolidate democracy and the rule of law, as well as respect for human rights and fundamental freedoms.

However, in order to pursue these ambitious objectives, the TEU gives the common institutions some simple **intergovernmental cooperation means** [see section 1.2.1]: defining the principles of and general guidelines for the common foreign and security policy; deciding on common strategies; adopting joint actions; adopting common positions; and strengthening systematic cooperation between the Member States in the conduct of policy (Art. 12 TEU). **Decisions** on CFSP matters are taken by the **Council acting unanimously** but any member of the Council may abstain in order to allow a decision to be taken. The "**constructive abstention**" allows some Member States not to participate in a joint action, thus making it easier to adopt initiatives which have a broad measure of support (two thirds of the weighted majority).

On matters not having military or defence implications, the Council **may act by qualified majority** [see section 5.2.6], when adopting a decision on the basis of a common strategy defined by the European Council, and when adopting any decision implementing a joint action or a common position (Art. 23 TEU). The possibility of a blocking veto remains, even for a common position or action to be taken in the framework of a common strategy, but a Member State has to offer an explanation for its use. Such explanations are not a deterrent of veto, if one Member State is determined to defend its interests, which diverge from those of the majority. It transpires that the CFSP method is an improved intergovernmental cooperation method, but not much more than that [see section 1.2.1]. Even if the improvements brought by the Constitutional Treaty were implemented [see sections 3.3.4 and 3.3.5], the foreign and security policy could not become a "common policy" by the means put at its disposal [see section 1.3.1].

6.4.6. What is the institutional framework of the common foreign and security policy?

The Secretary-General of the Council, who is the **High Representative for the CFSP**, assists the Council in those matters coming within the scope of the CFSP, by contributing in particular to the formulation, preparation and implementation of policy decisions and, at the request of the Presidency, by conducting political dialogue with third parties (Art. 26 TEU). **The Presidency** represents the Union in all matters falling within the CFSP [see section 4.1.2]. It is responsible for the implementation of common measures and expresses the position of the Union in international organisations and conferences. The Commission is closely involved in those tasks of the Presidency. The Presidency must consult the European Parliament on the main aspects and the basic choices of the CFSP and must ensure that its views are duly taken into consideration (Art. 21 TEU).

A **Political Committee** consisting of Political Directors of the Member States monitors the international situation in the areas covered by common foreign and security policy and contributes to the definition of policies by delivering opinions to the Council at the latter's request or on its own initiative. A **Policy Planning and Early Warning Unit**, under the responsibility of the Secretary-General of the Council has the following tasks: monitoring and analysing developments in areas relevant to the CFSP; providing assessments of the Union's foreign and security policy interests; providing early warning of events or situations which may have significant repercussions for the CFSP; producing policy options papers to be presented under the responsibility of the Presidency as a contribution to policy formulation in the Council.

6.4.7. What does the European security and defence policy entail?

Common foreign and security policy covers all questions related to the security of the European Union, including the **progressive framing of a European security and defence policy (ESDP)**, which might in time lead to a common defence, should the European Council so decide. The progressive framing of a common defence policy will be supported, when considered appropriate, by cooperation between the Member States in the field of armaments (Art. 17 TEU). This policy must be aimed in particular at reducing risks and uncertainties which could impair the territorial integrity and political independence of the Union and of its Member States, their democratic nature, their economic stability and the stability of the neighbouring regions.

For the time being, the Member States, at the Helsinki European Council (10-11 December 1999), have decided to develop capabilities and establish political and military structures for **conflict prevention and crisis management**, the so-called **Petersberg tasks.** To this end, the Union decided to have an autonomous capacity to take decisions and, where NATO as a whole is not engaged, to launch and then to conduct EU-led military operations in response to international crises. Cooperating together voluntarily, Member States should be able to deploy 60 000 men in less than 60 days and to sustain them for at least one year, for the purpose of EU-led conflict prevention and crisis management tasks. The "2010 **headline goal**" is the capability to deploy forces on the ground no later than 10 days after the decision to launch the operation.

To pursue the headline goal of the European Security and Defence policy, the following permanent **political and military bodies** have been established within the Council. A standing **Political and Security Committee (PSC)** in Brussels, composed of national representatives of senior/ambassadorial level, deals with all aspects of the CFSP, including the common European security and defence policy. The **Military Committee (MC)**, composed of the chiefs of defence or their military delegates, gives military advice, makes recommendations to the PSC and provides military direction to the Military Staff. The **Military Staff (MS)**, composed of military personnel seconded from Member States to the General Secretariat of the Council, provides military expertise and support to the ESDP, including the conduct of early warning, situation assessment and strategic planning for Petersberg tasks.

Article 17 (TEU) underlines that the policy of the Union does not prejudice the specific character of the security and defence policy of certain Member States, respects the obligations of certain Member States under the **North Atlantic Treaty Organisation (NATO)** and is compatible with the common security and defence policy established within that framework. For the Member States concerned, this means that the actions and decisions they undertake within the framework of EU military crisis management will respect at all times all their Treaty obligations as NATO allies. According to the Helsinki European Council, all Member States (defence ministers) are entitled to participate fully and on an equal footing in all decisions and deliberations of the Council and Council bodies on EU-led operations, but the commitment of national assets by Member States to such operations will be **based on their sovereign decision**. It is apparent that the European security and defence policy depends on intergovernmental cooperation [see section 1.2.1], is still in its infancy and is more or less under the tutelage of NATO.

6.4.8. What does the Constitutional Treaty provide for the common foreign and security policy?

The Constitution's principal amendment to the provisions of the Treaty on European Union was the institution of a **Union Minister for Foreign Affairs**, who would wear two hats, being both one of the Commission's Vice-Presidents and the President of the Foreign Affairs Council [see section 3.3.4]. This association of the Commission and the Council in the person of the Foreign Affairs Minister could be beneficial for the common foreign and security policy. Exercising the right of initiative of the Commission [see section 4.2.2], the Union Minister for Foreign Affairs would contribute to the development of the CFSP, which he or she would carry out as mandated by the Council. The same would apply to the common security and defence policy (Art I-28). He or she would have responsibilities incumbent on the Commission in external relations and for coordinating the CFSP with other aspects of the Union's external action (notably common commercial and aid to development policies) [see section 4.2.4].

According to the Constitutional Treaty, the Minister for Foreign Affairs would be in charge of a **European External Action Service** set up to assist the Minister in his or her functions (Article III-296). This service would be composed of officials from relevant departments of the General Secretariat of the Council of Ministers and of the Commission and staff seconded from national diplomatic services. This multinational service could develop into a real European diplomatic corps, a development which could enhance the image of the Union in the world and bring home the views of third countries on the EU as such rather than on its individual Member States.

The **European security and defence policy (ESDP)** would also be strengthened by the Constitutional Treaty. More missions would be added to the so-called Petersberg tasks [see section 6.4.7], such as joint disarmament operations, military advice and assistance tasks, conflict prevention and post-conflict stabilisation. A solidarity clause was introduced whereby the other Member States would provide assistance if a Member State was the victim of a terrorist attack or a natural or man-made disaster. In this case, the Union would mobilise all the instruments at its disposal, including the military resources made available by the Member States, in order to assist the Member State concerned (Article I-43). More important could be the **mutual defence clause** of the Constitution asserting that, if a Member State was the victim of armed aggression on its territory, the other Member States would have towards it an obligation of aid and assistance by all the means in their power, in accordance with Article 51 of the United Nations Charter (Article I-41(7).

However, the Constitution would mark **no real progress in terms of decision-making** in the area of the CFSP [see section 5.2.1]. The use of legislative instruments such as European laws and framework laws would be excluded [see section 5.3.3]. The Council of Ministers would continue to decide by unanimity in most cases and, therefore, Member States would still have the right of veto. By way of derogation from the unanimity rule, the Council would act by qualified majority [see section 5.2.6] only under certain strictly defined conditions (Art. III-300). This "switchover" from unanimity to qualified majority would not apply to decisions with military implications or in the area of defence. Moreover, any Member State could declare its intention to oppose the adoption of a decision by qualified majority. Hence, the foreign and security policies could not become "common", if just one State of the twenty-five did not want it [see section 7.2.5].

6.4.9. Has the political union of Europe marked any progress to date?

Common needs have pushed forward the **internal wing** of the political union stage [see section 6.4.3]. The Member States have understood that the common problems of external immigration, smuggling and terrorism could not be faced with separate policies. This perception of the need for a common policy has led to the effective disbanding of the so-called third pillar of the Union and to the placing of most subjects concerning it inside the basic trunk of the Community, managed by the Community decision-making procedure [see section 5.2.1].

This procedure does not apply to the **external wing** of political union, the so-called second pillar of the Union, i.e. the euphemistically called **common foreign and security policy**. The prevailing intergovernmental cooperation, even if improved by the Constitutional Treaty [see section 3.3.4], cannot lead to a really common policy [see section 1.3.1]. The very term "common foreign and security policy" is misleading. The citizens hear "common policy" and do not see anything resembling that [see sections 7.2.6 and 7.2.7]. If the Treaty called for cooperation in foreign and security policy, the citizens would at least understand better what is meant. Now, they rightly believe that they are derided when their political leaders speak about a common policy and at the first test of such a policy they hide behind their national interests (real or imaginary), in order to undermine it.

So as to start becoming a common policy, the **CFSP should be provided with the means of such a policy**, i.e. basically decision-making by the majority of the Member States and the population of the Union with full participation of the Commission, the Parliament, the European Court of Justice and specific organs [see section 5.2.6]. The snag in this development is that the political leaders in most Member States do not want to lose the power or the illusion of power that they hold through their national foreign and security policies, even if these have lost their effectiveness in a world run by a superpower. The citizens must comprehend this reality in order to force their political leaders to change it [see section 7.2.6]. The change and consequently the progress of Europe's political union can come about through a new Constitution [see section 7.2.4] or at least via enhanced cooperation [see section 5.2.7] of a core of Member States for a genuinely common foreign and security policy [see section 7.2.9].

Chapter 7

EUROPEAN INTEGRATION AND ITS OUTLOOK

Europe's history relates in the main the wars for the domination of some nations over the others and the battles of those others for their liberation from their oppressor or oppressors. After centuries of incessant wars, recurring aggressions, revolutions, massacres, human sacrifices, genocides, material destructions, economic disasters, Europe arrived in the middle of the last century at the most devastating war of world history, the economic downfall of all European nations and the world supremacy of a non-European power. Fortunately, however, right after the Second World War, some inspired politicians, like Schuman, Adenauer, De Gasperi and Spaak, realised that the European nations, which had just ruined each other in a nonsensical war for the enlargement of their economic space, were in fact parts of **a single geographic, economic and political entity**, that could guarantee the prosperity of all in a single market [see section 2.1.1].

7.1. An appraisal of European integration

7.1.1. Is the European model of integration working?

Fifty years after the "invitation to union" of Robert Schuman we may say with confidence that the expectations of the fathers of European unification have been largely fulfilled. The European Community/Union has built the three first floors of its edifice – the customs union, the common market and economic and monetary union – and although work is still needed and done daily on them, it has started building the last floor, that of political union. Work at one wing of this floor, that of home and judicial policy, is advancing satisfactorily. The big question is if and when work will get started on the wing of foreign and security policy [see section 6.4.9].

The work already accomplished qualifies the European model as **a success story**. Multinational integration has established peace in Western Europe, has turned the former enemies into good partners, has secured the equality of all participating nations under common laws, has ensured development opportunities and thus the relative prosperity of all. In short, the European Community/Union has become an island of peace and prosperity in a world that is, unfortunately, still suffering from skilfully cultivated ethnic, racial, religious and other differences, battles for the glory of warmongers, the slaughter and displacement of populations for ethnic and/or economic reasons and, finally, the exploitation of the vast majority of mankind by an unscrupulous minority, equally distributed among various nations.

7.1.2. What are the proofs of the success of the European integration model?

The course of the multinational integration process in the European Community/Union is determined by **three currents that converge at certain points** and strengthen the main flow: (a) the increasing number of the participants; (b) the continuous raising of their goals through the passage from one integration stage to another; and (c) the constant increase of their activities by the development of common policies.

The membership has kept growing together with the tasks assumed by the team. The multinational integration process began in 1951 as a customs union concerning only the coal and steel sectors of six countries on the basis of the ECSC Treaty [see sections 2.1 and 3.1.1]. In 1958, these same countries extended the operation of the customs union and of the common market to all the sectors of their economies, thanks to the EEC Treaty [see section 3.1.2]. In 1973, they were joined by three countries, which had originally preferred intergovernmental cooperation inside a free trade area [see sections 1.2.1, 2.1.2 and 2.2]. In 1992, the builders of the common market had become twelve, had completed the work on that stage of their integration on the basis of the Single European Act and had signed the Treaty of Maastricht leading them to the next stage of their integration [see section 3.2.1]. In 1995, the builders of the union were joined by three more states, which had originally believed in the benefits of the free trade area. At the turn of the century, the fifteen were finalising their economic and monetary union, were progressing in their political union thanks to the Treaty of Amsterdam and were opening the door of their enterprise to ten more states [see section 2.2].

Despite the successive enlargements, the multinational integration process in Europe has followed **a steady evolution in stages of ever closer convergence** - customs union, common market, economic and monetary union - and is proceeding towards the final stage of political union. The **customs union**, nowadays taken for granted and almost forgotten, formed the solid foundation of the entire European edifice [see section 6.1]. The problem-free removal of customs barriers to trade filled the apprentices of European construction with the enthusiasm necessary for climbing up the steep and unfamiliar road of integration. The stage of the **common market**, completed in 1992, meant the freedom of movement within the single market of goods, persons, services and capital [see section 6.2]. These freedoms revolutionised trade and competition, the working methods and the economic conditions in the Member States of the Community [see section 6.2.2]. They also opened the way for a single currency. Thus, in December 1991 in Maastricht, the Member States decided to initiate the next stage of their integration, viz. **economic and monetary union (EMU)**, implying a single monetary policy, necessary for the management of a single currency, and the convergence of national economic policies [see section 6.3].

The preceding summary of events and trends demonstrates the **extraordinary success of the multinational integration process** as practised in Europe since the early 1950s. This success was due to the construction method taught by Schuman and Monnet, which is that of a step by step advance after careful evaluation of the previous experience [see section 1.2.1]. Brick upon brick, act after act, as taught by the old masters, the European edifice has been built up and is still growing. Every new measure fits so well into the adjoining provisions that it fills a gap while consolidating the whole structure. In fact, the successful formula of European integration is based on **common policies** [see section 1.3] built by **common institutions** [see chapter 4] following the **Community method** [see section 5.2.1].

If the supreme interests of the citizens of the participating states are the assurance of peace with their neighbours and the increase of their wellbeing, the common policies of the European Community/Union have served those interests well. They have **transformed the former enemies into partners**. War between the members of the Union has become unthinkable and the wellbeing of their citizens has greatly increased through the constant development of their economies and through the abundance of good quality products and services inside the single market. In addition, the common policies attain a great number of lesser common goals. They monitor the free exchange of industrial and agricultural goods between the Member States. They stimulate and support the development of the poorer regions of the Union. They guarantee the rights of the citizens of the Member States to travel, to live and to work wherever they choose within its territory. Certainly, none of these policies is perfect, but all of them are under the constant scrutiny of the common institutions and they are amended very often, in order to be adapted to the new needs that emerge inside or outside the Union [see section 1.3.4].

7.1.3. What are the most important shortcomings of European integration to date?

The most important failure of European institutions to date is their **poor contact with the citizens**. European citizens feel that the Union is influencing their lives and that they are left in the dark by the European institutions and their own political leaders as to its workings. They show their indignation about this state of affairs in European elections, referendums and opinion polls. The information deficit is, indeed, more responsible for the estrangement of the citizens from the European integration process than the much decried democratic deficit [see section 5.2.5]. It is also worsening even as the integration process is deepening and encompassing an ever-growing number of economic, societal and political sectors.

If the citizens were led to believe that the disadvantages of integration were greater than its benefits, they might be led to press their political leaders to disengage their country or countries from the integration process or to halt this process altogether. If we consider the effects of the information deficit on some referenda, in the past (the Danish concerning the Treaty of Maastricht, the Irish concerning the Treaty of Nice and the French and Dutch concerning the Constitutional Treaty) [see section 7.1.7], this scenario is not as absurd as it seems at first glance. In a community of people, where a silent majority has no interest in the common affairs and goals, while a determined minority is strongly opposed to its objectives and institutions, there is a strong probability that the minority group would tend to grow over time and to become stronger and ever more convinced of its ideas and ideals. Unopposed by the silent majority, it might thus eventually succeed in reversing the working system that holds the community together.

A paradoxical effect of the information and civic deficit about European integration is that, while citizens seem to be indifferent to the European Union, they simultaneously expect ever more important results from it. This is notably the case concerning the **European presence on the world stage**, the second serious flaw of the European edifice. Eurobarometer surveys indicate that two in three Europeans believe that the European Union should have a truly common foreign policy [see section 7.2.6].

The citizens' expectations for a powerful Union in the world include the dissemination and defence of the European ideals of peace, welfare, democracy, the rule of law and social justice on the world stage. Europe is open to the world and its citizens understand that they cannot live merrily in a prosperous island surrounded by the misery and envy of other nations. They understand that, for their own wellbeing, peace and security, the Union should contribute more to peace and sustainable development in the world. Europeans know as well that they cannot prevent the new technologies and free enterprise from shrinking the world to the virtual dimensions of a village; but they feel that this, as any village, should have a town hall and that they should have their representatives inside it. In other words, they expect the Union to play **an active role in the globalisation phenomenon** by enhancing the legitimacy and effectiveness of international institutions, notably the United Nations and its specialised agencies, so that these may impose the law in the fields of global environment protection, peace, durable development, social protection, commerce and competition.

Europeans fail to understand how the economic giant that they have created, the most important power in international trade, now endowed with the strongest currency in the world, **cannot make its voice heard in the world arena**. They expect the Union to take the lead in monitoring regional conflicts, globalisation, environmental challenges and famines in the world. The tragic inability of the Union to prevent the Balkan wars at its doorstep or to enforce the rules of international law in the resolution of conflicts in the Middle East has greatly reduced the respect of Europeans for their common institutions. Public reasoning is quite simple: as long as the Union cannot act as a mature political giant, it cannot be respected. It is time for the infant giant to grow up.

7.1.4. Do citizens appreciate the European integration model?

The citizens are silent, but indispensable, actors in the construction of Europe. The EC/EU could not have been built by the political elite, without the implicit consent of the citizens involved in the process. In fact, European citizens are generally in favour and consider as evident the fundamental principles and ideals the Union stands for, notably peace among their previously antagonistic nations, respect for human rights and the rule of law, economic development and social protection. The **public opinion survey known as "Eurobarometer"**, which is conducted each spring and autumn under the auspices of the Commission, shows that, in the end of 2004, EU citizens (from the 25 member states) were largely convinced that EU membership was a "good " rather than a "bad thing" (56% vs. 13%). 50% of the citizens had a positive image of the EU, compared to 15% who had a bad image. 52% of the respondents in the 25 countries had confidence in the European Commission (-27%) and 57% had confidence in the European Parliament. It is interesting to note that good information greatly enhances the positive attitude of the public towards European integration. Two out of three citizens who claim to be well informed have a positive image of the EU as against one out of three who admit to being ill informed. Three out of four citizens would like to be better informed about the EU and 85% support the notion that children should be taught in school about the way European Union institutions work. Civic education on EU institutions is even the first priority theme for the very large majority of Europeans. Apparently, the citizens are aware that something important is happening in Europe, in which they cannot participate for lack of general knowledge and day-to-day information and they call for better access to European affairs for themselves and their children.

The information deficit, acknowledged by the citizens themselves, means that they are ill informed about the reasons, the goals and the achievements of European policies, laws and measures. Ignorance brings disregard for the obscure phenomenon. At best, citizens take for granted or fail to see that the EC/EU is behind the many rights that they have acquired thanks to European integration, particularly the right to a peaceful, liberal and law secured existence. For uninformed Europeans, the peaceful coexistence and emulation of different European nations is self-evident and not to be attributed to unfamiliar Treaties, policies or common legislation.

7.1.5. To what is the information deficit of European citizens due?

The information deficit originates from the early days of the customs union and the common market, when the issues of European unification were too technical to really interest the public and the threat of the communist block was considered a sufficient justification of this unification. Now that the communist threat has disappeared and the evolutionary integration process generates, every day, new common policies and laws affecting all sectors of the economy and society of the Member States, the citizens are bewildered about their impact on their lives. Furthermore, in order to judge the common enterprise on its true advantages and disadvantages, they **need to have matter-of-fact information** on the existing and anticipated benefits and drawbacks as well as on the real management difficulties that it is facing.

The information deficit is **partly due to the European institutions**, notably the Commission, the Council and the Parliament, which do not join their forces to build a common communication policy. In their defence, it may be said that they are not encouraged - if they are not discouraged - by **the governments of the Member States**, which do not feel that they have a common interest in setting up a common information policy. In order to assume the political credit of modernisation, governments, when proposing innovating laws to national parliaments, transposing in effect Community directives, or when changing their administrative practices to comply with Community law, rarely take the trouble to explain to the general public that they are thus fulfilling their Community obligations. If the Community measure is popular, governments will tend to present as their own initiative the national law or decree implementing the Community decision, hardly mentioning the common framework of the action. On the contrary, if the measure is unpopular, "Brussels" is often made responsible by the governments of the Member States for an action that they have themselves adopted (in the Council) [see section 5.2.4] or even encouraged (in the European Council).

7.1.6. What are the dangers of the information deficit of European citizens?

Actually, **the Commission is the main provider of information on the EC/EU.** Major European affairs and problems, which occasionally attract television attention, are presented and commented in the press room of the Commission by its President, the competent Commissioner or a spokesperson. Rarely is press attention focused on the European Parliament and almost never on the Council of Ministers. Although it practically monopolises Community information, **the Commission is not a secretive organisation** and is even a good provider of information, as far as its activities are concerned. Its Representations in the capitals and other major cities of the Member States are open to the interested public. Its Office of Official Publications (EUR-OP) publishes hundreds of documents every year on all common policies. Its Europa server on the Internet gives free and user-friendly access to more than 60 databases, each of which contains several hundred thousand documents in all Community languages.

A cursory view of the information activities of European institutions gives the impression of **a flood of documentation** - coming mainly from the Commission - rather than of an information drought. But floods can be more harmful than droughts, if the soil is not prepared to receive the overflow. In this case, the soil is totally unprepared, because the citizens do not and never will make an effort to get the existing information, but rightly expect that they will be automatically informed, through their familiar media, about European affairs and decisions that are of interest to them. When they say in Eurobarometer surveys that they want to be informed about the institutions and policies of the EU [see section 7.1.4], they mean that this **information should come to them**, not that they should go after it. Useful as they are to interested persons (researchers, interest groups and other specialists), the Commission publications and Internet sites are ignored and are therefore useless for the large majority of citizens.

The result of information deficiency, combined with disinformation on the part of eurosceptic media, is **the indifference or, worse, the dissatisfaction of citizens**, who quite sincerely believe that, instead of progressing in the field of European unification, the European Union is a theatre of infighting among European politicians. Not only all governments but also all major political parties, which are generally pro-integration, should recognize that the information deficit covered by a systematic disinformation on the part of some europhobic media is **undermining the common policies** that they want to carry through [see section 1.3], is debasing the democratic institutions set up and empowered by them to implement those common policies [see chapter 4] and is halting the progress of European integration [see section 7.1.3].

The European institutions and the governments of the Member States should acknowledge that **a common information policy**, which might have been a luxury as long as the integration process was confined to customs and technical matters [see section 6.1], is a necessity now that the process is spreading ever more from the purely economic to the political field [see section 1.3.4]. A common information and communication policy should cover all the activities of the European institutions and should be implemented by a European Press Agency in close cooperation with the governments of the Member States. Such a common communication policy, combined with the civic education of young Europeans at school, **would bring the citizens closer to the Union** and would secure the achievements of all the other common policies.

7.1.7. Can referendums on the ratification of European Treaties bring citizens closer to the integration process?

First of all, it is highly unusual that a treaty, be it called constitutional, be subject to a referendum for its ratification. Treaties are negotiated and signed by governments and they are ratified by them after the assent of their parliaments. This is the case because **treaties are very complicated legal instruments** that cannot be well understood by ordinary citizens. European treaties are even more complicated than average international treaties. They contain not only new elements, necessary for bringing the integration process forward, but also all the previous provisions on which the construction of the existing stages of the integration process was based, notably customs union, the common market and economic and monetary union [see section 3.2]. It is absurd to ask citizens to approve or reject a new instrument that contains some new measures promoting the integration process and all the pre-existing measures on which this process has been based since half a century.

The referendum on a new treaty should either concern exclusively the new provisions of this treaty compared to those in effect or, if it also concerns the provisions in force, should allow the citizens of a Member State to opt for the secession of their country from the Union, if they are not satisfied with its ends or results. If the subject of the referendum is not made that clear, it would give the opportunity to demagogues at both extremes of the political spectrum to deprecate not just the new elements of the integration process, but also elements of the acquis communautaire [see section 5.1.4], like the European social model or the common agricultural policy, which function satisfactorily in the opinion of the majority of the Member States. With the information deficit that prevails, demagogues are free to disseminate all sorts of lies on the European Union and to exert a negative influence on public opinion. It is contrary to the concept of democracy to have the citizens decide on the basis of **lies, which thanks to propaganda, they have accepted as truths** [see section 7.1.4]. Hence, a referendum may estrange rather than bring the citizens closer to the integration process.

Moreover, it is highly undemocratic to ask only the citizens of some Member States to express themselves directly by referendum, whereas the citizens from the other Member States should be contented with the normal procedure of the ratification approved by thei representatives in the national parliaments. This is **discrimination between citizens of the Member States**, condemned in principal by the Treaty itself [see section 5.2.5]. Democratic considerations and the principle of the equality of the citizens of the Union require that they all express themselves on the ratification of a new treaty in the same way: either indirectly through their representatives or directly through referenda held the same day in all countries, so that the results in one country do not influence the citizens of the others. If the second alternative was preferred, the governments and the common institutions should make a greater effort at informing the citizens about the issues at stake.

Instead of submitting a complex legal instrument to the approval or disapproval of the citizens, it would be more logical to offer them **a small briefing paper** highlighting the new elements of the treaty, describing them in a non legalistic language, explaining why the responsible governments have agreed to them by signing the treaty and asking them if they want this new treaty to be ratified and be brought into force or if they want to leave things as they are with the existing treaty. All the governments concerned should agree to such a straightforward paper at the same time as they sign the new treaty (constitutional or not), so that the citizens of all Member States have the same explanations and reasons for the new elements of the common enterprise and are asked the same questions about its progress or standstill [see section 7.2.4]. It would, indeed, be hypocritical and improper for a government to put its signature on a draft treaty (which is in fact a draft contract with its partners) and present it in a different way from its partners, knowing or hopping that its citizens will reject it.

7.2. The outlook of European integration

7.2.1. What are the big challenges facing the European integration process?

European integration by itself cannot solve all the economic and social problems of the Member States. Integration is only an instrument for building an internal market by consensual methods between formerly antagonistic nations. The large internal market is useful for developing trade and other transactions between the Member States and through them for raising the living standards of the populations concerned [see section 6.2.1]. It is also necessary for providing businesses with conditions of competition similar to those prevailing in other competing large markets, notably the US, Japan, China and India. Upon the internal market was built the European social model, i.e. high standards of social justice and protection for the populations taking part in the integration process. The internal market and the single currency shield more than 60% of European agricultural, industrial and commercial transactions from outside competition [see section 6.3.1]. But for transactions with the rest of the world, Europe must find common answers to the common problem of **preserving employment with high social standards for its citizens**, while competing with countries with lower or no such standards.

The globalisation phenomenon and the lowering of tariff barriers inside the World Trade Organisation (WTO) have practically eliminated the protection of European production and are even displacing production from Europe to low wage and low or no social protection countries. This is certainly good for the development of these countries, but it is endangering production and living standards in Europe. Hence, the European social model is more and more threatened by nations practising social dumping, i.e. providing workers with hardly the means of subsistence and low or no social protection. In a common market where products from third countries can enter a port in one Member State and therefrom find their way to the markets of all the others [see section 6.2.3], the solution to the common problem can only be found in **common economic and commercial policies**. This is a major challenge facing European political leaders [see section 6.3.10].

Moreover, Europe is rightly seen as a haven of peace and prosperity by the citizens of third countries who are living below subsistence levels. They try by all legal and illegal means to enter this haven and to live in dignity if not in affluence inside it. This again is good for them, but there is a limit to the immigrant populations which Europe can accommodate on its small territory without endangering the economic, social, cultural and even political standards of its own citizens. The problem is common to all Member States, since the immigrants entering legally or illegally into one of them can then move and settle in any other [see section 6.2.4]. Hence, common solutions, aiming at reception of such immigrants and at developing the countries from which they come, have to be found. Only a **really common foreign policy** combining all the forces of the Twenty-five can meet this and other challenges coming from outside the European Union.

It should be stressed that the economic unification of Europe has taken half a century in order to attain the present adequately advanced stage of integration, with economic and monetary union. Moreover, economic integration began with six clearly europhilic nations [see section 2.1]. The stage of political union now concerns four times as many Member States, many of which are not europhilic, as they prefer to slow down rather than to speed up the integration process. Moreover, the political interests of the Member States, on which common policies should be built [see section 1.3.3], are, at least for the time being, even more different than their economic interests. In view of these facts, the political union of Europe needs to be written urgently in a new charter, whether this be called **a Constitution or a largely amended Treaty**. Since the Constitutional Treaty signed in October 2004 will probably never come into force, the political leaders of Europe should very soon start preparing a new Treaty, constitutional or not [see section 7.2.4].

7.2.2. Can European integration be expected to develop in the future?

The common policies, which materialise European integration, are there to meet the societal needs which arise in a defined community of nations at a given time. Therefore, not only the objectives which the member states set for each common policy, but also the means which they give to the common institutions to attain them and the measures which the latter adopt to implement them change in accordance with the economic, political and social needs which the participant states experience at a certain time. In the case of the EC/EU, the common policies are **in permanent evolution**, demonstrated, for all of them, by the constant amendment of the Community laws (regulations, directives, etc.) that form them, and, for some of them, by the amendment of the Treaty provisions that concern them. Moreover, a common policy tends to spill over onto the area of other common policies, to produce needs, to cause reactions and to nourish their development [see section 1.3.4].

The constant evolution of all common policies causes the endless evolution of the multinational integration process [see section 1.2.1]. The development of common policies creates ever-stronger economic and political links between the peoples of Europe. Paradoxically, the constant progress of integration in all fields demonstrates both the soundness of the Community model and the imperfection of this model. An organisation and a process that are in a state of permanent evolution can never be perfect. They may only be improved. The "**constant progress syndrome**" is the strong point and the permanent challenge of the European model of integration. The simple answer to the question above is that European integration will normally keep developing over time, trying to reach an integration ideal that it will never attain, since ideals, by definition, can never be totally attained.

7.2.3. Can the European Union overcome the crisis brought about by the rejection of the Constitution?

When signing the Treaty of Nice, in 2000, the governments of the Fifteen knew that this was a transitory Treaty, enabling the EC/EU to function temporarily with the expected addition of ten new members [see section 3.2.3]. Being temporary, this Treaty was not expected to allow the EC/EU to progress beyond its present state of development. Keen to push ahead with the integration process, the heads of State or Government called for a new Intergovernmental Conference to prepare a new treaty and then, in December 2001, decided to convene a Convention to draft a "constitutional treaty", which they signed in October 2004 [see section 3.3.1]. But, this draft constitutional treaty had a major flaw. **It required all the Member States to ratify it** in order to come into force, allowing even those that wished to do so to put this ratification to a referendum [see section 3.3.5]. In fact, the citizens of France and the Netherlands, on 29 May and 1 June 2005 respectively, have rejected the draft Constitution for reasons strange to the Constitution itself. They have thus, probably unknowingly and unwillingly, brought a crisis to the functioning of the institutions and to the progress of the integration process [see section 7.1.7].

But this crisis is probably temporary. The major reason for this optimistic presumption is that, contrary to what is believed or hoped by eurosceptics, the non ratification of the Constitutional Treaty will not undo the concrete achievements of European integration and will not bring it back to the intergovernmental cooperation of a free trade area [see sections 1.2.1 and 6.1.1]. The European Union has already advanced well into the integration stages of the customs union, the common market and economic and monetary union [see chapter 6]. It has already achieved an impressive “acquis communautaire”, i.e. common legislation that binds the Member States together [see section 5.1.1]. The great majority of the political and economic elite of these States are convinced that the European integration model works and gives better results than a free trade area like the EFTA, which is practically absorbed into the EC/EU. The citizens of these States enjoy the freedoms and the social protection that the European model provides [see section 6.2.2]. In their great majority, the citizens of most European countries want European integration to advance to the stage of political union, through the realisation of a functional common foreign and security policy [see section 7.2.6]. All these facts show that the majority of Europeans want to move forward, not backward.

Moreover, all common policies function normally and require everyday decisions to be taken by the institutions. Even if decision-making is admittedly difficult in the current institutional and legal context, economic, societal and political needs require that decisions be taken [see section 1.3.4]. The pressure of existing common policies and the demand of the majority of citizens of most Member States for a really common foreign and security policy will oblige the political leaders to sit down again at the negotiating table to draft a **new Constitution or at least a Treaty replacing the existing Treaties** on the European Community and on the European Union. The new Constitution or the new Treaty may incorporate all the important institutional innovations contained in the Constitutional Treaty signed in October 2004, since they have already been agreed by the governments of all Member States, with two big differences - the decision-making procedure of the common foreign and security policy [see section 7.2.7] and the ratification of this Constitution or Treaty [see section 7.2.4]. They should both be based on the majority principle and not on the unanimity of the participants.

7.2.4. Can the European Union have a Constitution?

The experience of the Constitutional Treaty should lead the debate on a possible European Constitution. The faults committed in the drafting and in the handing over of this Treaty to the people should be avoided [see section 3.3.5 and 7.1.7]. The citizens of the Member States should be involved in the drafting of the Constitution. This Constitution should satisfy the aspirations of European peoples to see their Union become a major actor on the international stage [see section 7.2.6]. It should reinforce the institutional framework of the Union so that the latter may function effectively in an increasingly complex internal and external environment. The Constitution should be put to ratification in a homogeneous way in all member countries, either by the national parliaments or by a referendum organised the same day in all Member States, after adequate explication of its contents. The Constitution should provide that only willing nations should adopt it and offer an alternative for those that do not want to do so.

All these requirements lead to the following suggestion. The European Council should convoke a **constituent assembly**. This could be made up of the members of the European Parliament elected by the peoples of the Union with this specific mandate in addition to their normal legislative mission [see section 4.3.2]. Prior to this election, a large public debate should take place in all Member States at the initiative of political parties. All options for the future of Europe should be aired. The candidates for the election to the assembly should expose their position on all the big issues of European politics. Consequently, the citizens of each State would have the option of sending to the assembly europhilic or eurosceptic representatives. The majority of the assembly would thus be constituted by europhilic or eurosceptic members regardless of their traditional political preferences. Of course, these preferences would also direct the debates in the assembly on many issues, such as human rights, social protection or free competition to be guaranteed by the Constitution.

If the majority of the assembly were constituted by eurosceptic members, it could turn down the drafting of a Constitution or restrain the integration process through it. If, on the contrary, the majority of the constituent assembly were made up of europhilic members, **it could reinforce and speed up the integration process**, particularly in the field of foreign and security policy. In any case, the outcome of the debates in the assembly would have a democratic legitimacy, since it would correspond to the will of the majority of the peoples of the Union. The draft Constitution should then be agreed and signed by the heads of State or Government of the Union.

The most important Article of the Constitution would be the one dealing with **the ratification procedure** [see section 3.3.5]. It would be up to the members of the constituent assembly to decide if the ratification should depend on the agreement of the parliaments of the Member States or of the citizens themselves through a referendum [see section 7.1.7]. But, in both cases, the ratification procedure should be homogeneous and give each Member State the possibility to either ratify and, therefore, accept the coming into force of the Constitution or reject ratification and, thus, be excluded from the integration process. Hence, the Constitution should come into force and be binding only for those nations that have signed and ratified it.

Instead of the absurd and anti-democratic condition of ratification by all Member States - by reason of which the will of one may prevail over the determination of all the others - the new Constitution should allow its coming into force after the **ratification by a large majority of the signatories**, e.g. four fifths of the Member States representing four fifths of the population of the Union. The problem will thus be transferred from the large majority of the Member States, which want to advance in their Union and are slowed down by the laggards, to the latter, who will realise that, if they do not march in step with the group, they will stay behind and they will have either to run to catch up or stay out of it. This is the Gordian knot, which should be cut, since it cannot be unfastened, by the majority of the Member States. The geopolitical circumstances, which place the divided European nations in the margin of world affairs, will force them to do it sooner than later.

7.2.5. Can the governance of the Union become more democratic?

"**European governance**" - i.e., the rules, processes and behaviour of the actors that affect the way in which powers are exercised at European level - has worked relatively well up to now, since it has made possible all the achievements of the common policies of the integration process. Therefore, the role of the existing institutions should not be radically changed, nor should new institutions be added, because the rules of the functioning of the protagonists of European integration might be altered, with unknown consequences [see chapter 4]. However, European governance **has already**

reached its limits of efficiency, even if the improvements brought about by the Constitutional Treaty were implemented [see section 3.3.4]. It is doubtful that it could function efficiently in a union of twenty-five - and soon more - Member States, which could in addition have the ambition to deepen their political union. In order to enable the Union to better face internal and external challenges, a future reform of the institutions, brought about by an amendment of the existing Treaties [see section 3.2.3] or of a future Constitution [see section 7.2.4], should aim at their increased efficiency, legitimacy and rapprochement with the citizens of the Union.

The structure of the European Commission, in particular, should be democratised in parallel with the reinforcement of its role [see section 4.2.]. The actual handicap of the Commission is its technocratic character, due to the fact that the Commissioners are not elected but are appointed by the governments of the Member States [see section 4.2.1]. If the problem were stated in such simple terms, its solution would also be simple. It would be to **entrust the citizens themselves with the election of the members of the Commission** at the occasion of European elections. At the same time as they would choose the members of the European Parliament, the voters of each country could elect the Commissioner having the nationality of this country from a short list of candidates prepared by the national parliament. With this system of election in two phases, the national parliaments would play an important role in selecting (by successive votes) two or three personalities capable of assuming European functions, but the Commissioner for each nationality would finally be elected by the citizens of each nation (with the simple majority of the votes cast).

The president of the Commission and the vice-president, who could also be the Union Minister for Foreign Affairs (according to the Constitutional treaty) [see section 3.3.4 and 6.4.8], should be chosen from among these elected personalities by the European Council [see section 4.1.1], acting by qualified majority [see section 5.2.6], and be elected by the European Parliament (as provided for in the Constitutional treaty). The big difference between the system proposed here and the actual system or the one set forth in the Constitution is that the **president and the vice-president of the Commission would first be elected** by their respective countrymen and then would be chosen by the majority of the representatives of the peoples of the Union. They would not come out of the sole inspiration of the heads of State or government and would thus have a double democratic legitimacy, national and European. The European Parliament should also have a strong opinion on the suitability of the members of the Commission for the posts assigned to them by the President of this institution.

With such a system of democratic designation of Commissioners, the citizens would have an important incentive to elect strong personalities as members of the European executive organ, hoping that their compatriot could qualify for a top job, including that of the president or vice-president of the Commission. Moreover, **the citizens would feel that they participate in the governance of the Union**, since they would elect directly not only the members of one branch of the legislative authority (the European Parliament) [see section 4.3.1], but also the members of the executive authority (the European Commission).

Moreover, the European Parliament should play an important role, not only in the investiture of the executive authority of the Union, but also in its monitoring. In addition to the legality of the actions of the Commissioners, the Parliament should permanently control their independence in respect of their country of origin and their efficiency in the implementation of their pre-approved work programme. **The political role of the European Parliament would thus resemble that of a national parliament**, which controls the government of its country. At the same time, the legislative power of the Parliament - through the ordinary legislative procedure [see section 5.2.4] - should be extended to all legislative fields, including that of the **foreign and security policy,** which could thus, little by little, become a real common policy and propel the Union on the world scene [see section 7.2.7].

7.2.6. Do European citizens want a common foreign and security policy?

According to the Eurobarometer survey of public opinion in the twenty-five Member States of the EU, carried out in November/December 2004 and published in May 2005, **69% of European citizens support the concept of a common foreign policy** [see section 6.4.5]. In some countries – Belgium, Slovenia, Germany and Greece – the support for a common foreign policy is above 80%. The United Kingdom is the only country with a score of less than 50% (47%) in favour of the concept. 83% of the citizens of the Twenty-five would like, when an international crisis occurs, EU member states to agree on a common position. 82% affirm that EU foreign policy should be independent of the United States' foreign policy. 71% agree that the EU should have its own seat on the United Nations Security Council. 67% assert that the EU should have its own Foreign Minister who can be the spokesperson for a common European Union position.

Support of the citizens is even greater for a common security and defence policy (CSDP) [see section 6.4.7]. **78% of the citizens of the Twenty-five back a real CSDP** and support reaches almost 90% in Belgium, Slovenia and Germany. Even in the United Kingdom and Finland support for CSDP comes up to 60%. The lowest support for this policy (still around 55%) is among citizens of the traditionally neutral countries - Ireland and Sweden. The majority of citizens (52%) consider that the European Union is better placed than national governments (22%) to make decisions in the area of European defence policy. In the UK these percentages are 34 and 29 respectively.

Almost 60% of the respondents declare that they are in favour of a **European political union**, i.e. the last stage of European integration, and only 28% are against such a union [see section 6.4.1]. Only in Denmark, Finland, Sweden and the United Kingdom is the proportion of citizens against political union greater than that of those in favour. In all other countries, half to two thirds of the citizens support political union. In most of the new Member States as well as in Greece, Belgium and Italy, about 75% of the citizens support the development of the Union towards the stage of political union.

The responses of the citizens of the Fifteen and now of the Twenty-five to these questions have been practically the same over a long period of years, demonstrating that they are not motivated by the geopolitical situation of the moment, but are firmly embedded in their ideals for European integration. There is no question that the vast majority of European citizens **want their integration to progress to the stage of political union**, including a strong and independent foreign policy and an even stronger and more independent security and defence policy. Why do citizens understand that in an era of integration, globalisation and world predominance of a superpower, national sovereignty in matters of foreign policy and security has no real meaning, while their political leaders fail to understand this? Because, for the latter, national sovereignty is tantamount to their own power, which they do not want to share with their partners, even though this power is waning and only unity can bolster it [see section 1.2.1]. For this reason, a constituent assembly may respond better to the wishes of European citizens than their own political leaders. It may thus set objectives and guidelines in the Constitution for a really common foreign and security policy [see section 7.2.4].

The economic integration of Europe was promoted by economic interest groups [see section 1.1.3]. **The political integration should be promoted by the citizens themselves**. The citizens can and should indicate to the politicians, through political parties and the civil society, that they want Europe to have a common and independent foreign policy. Therefore, the citizens should be aware of the price to be paid for the achievement of a common policy, i.e. the new and important conferrals of national sovereignties to the common institutions [see sections 1.2.1, 2.1.2 and 3.3.2]. They should not have the illusion that they can have it both ways. They should be aware that the concept of a common policy implies that the solution to a common problem preferred by the majority may sometimes contravene what the citizens of one or a few States consider as a national interest. They should realize that, even if this could happen in one case, their national interests in general are better served by a European rather than by a national foreign policy. This awareness needs correct information and education of the citizens by the political elite, as well as their release from the sirens of nationalistic demagogy [see section 7.1.6], things admittedly difficult to achieve, particularly in eurosceptic nations.

7.2.7. How can the foreign and security policy become a real common policy?

Actually **the CFSP is based on intergovernmental cooperation**. This means that unanimity is required to make decisions in these fields, that the European Parliament does not participate in the decision-making process, that the Commission is not required to execute the decisions taken by the legislative organs and that the Court of Justice is not competent to settle disputes and control the legality of the decisions taken [see sections 1.2.1 and 5.2]. Any Member State may block a common position or common action on an important matter, thus frustrating the will of all the others [see section 6.4.6]. Moreover, any Member State may eventually disengage itself from a decision taken, thus effectively bringing to an end a common action agreed upon. Obviously, the foreign and security policy cannot become "common" as long as it depends on intergovernmental cooperation [see sections 6.4.5 and 6.4.9].

The coming into force of the **Constitutional Treaty would slightly improve** the decision-making procedure of the CFSP, but would not change fundamentally its intergovernmental character. It excludes the ordinary legislative procedure in matters of so-called common foreign and security policy, but requires it in matters concerning all the Union's other common policies [see sections 5.2.4 and 6.4.8]. In fact, European decisions relating to CFSP should be adopted by the European Council and the Council of Ministers unanimously, except when they are implementing decisions of the European Council taken unanimously or if the European Council unanimously decides that the Council of Ministers should act by qualified majority (Art. I-40, 6,7). All this means that, even if and when the Constitutional Treaty was adopted, the CFSP would be run by intergovernmental procedure and no common action or position could be taken, should one or just a few countries not want it. Hence, a really common foreign and security policy cannot exist, even with the improvements brought by the Constitutional Treaty.

To become a really common policy, the CFSP should be integrated into the Community pillar governed by the Community decision-making process [see section 5.2.1] or, better still, that the construction of the Union in pillars [see section 3.2.1] should be abandoned and **the Union be considered as a single structure**. The European Commission should be involved in the CFSP both at the stage of the initiative for common action and at the stage of execution of the decisions taken by the decision-making authorities. The European Parliament should be involved in decision-making, both by agreeing on the common strategies initiated by the European Council and by laying down European laws and framework laws with the Council of Ministers. European strategies and European laws and framework laws [see section 5.3.3] should be taken by qualified majority [see section 5.2.6], even if this majority were set at higher levels than those applying to other common policies, in order to make sure that a vast majority of the Member States, representing the great majority of the population of the Union agreed on a common strategy or a common action.

To assume its responsibilities as a global power, the EU should **rule out the use of unanimity and hence of the veto** in the common foreign and security policy. This policy should be given the necessary resources (budget, efficient procedures, network of external delegations, etc.). The actual functions of the High Representative for the CFSP and of the Commissioner for External Relations [see section 6.4.6] should be merged into the tasks of the Minister for Foreign Affairs (envisaged by the Constitutional Treaty) [see section 6.4.8], ensuring coherent single representation of collective EU external interests, a leading role in crisis management and consistency with other common policies such as trade and aid to development. Finally, the two wings of the foreign and security policy should back each other and make a coherent whole, because a foreign policy that cannot be enforced cannot be respected.

The same considerations apply to the common defence policy. The Community decision-making method [see section 5.2.1] should be applied to the **European security and defence policy (ESDP)** [see section 6.4.7], thus making it really common and truly European. The ESDP should be based on a common armament policy, which could rationalise, boost and make more competitive the armaments industries of the Member States. This could mean, *inter alia*, that the single market and common commercial policy could be applied to the defence industries. This integration could alleviate the current deficiencies of European military capabilities in the field of intelligence, logistics, communications and air transport systems. Effective public procurement and standardisation of armaments industries could help restructure, rationalise and strengthen European defence. If Europe realised its full defence potential, it would be ready to assume its role as a global player.

Europe can easily build up its power by bringing together the distinct and often overlapping **military capabilities of the Member States**. The existing military capabilities and military bodies of ESDP would only need to be strengthened and would be completely self-sufficient inside NATO. The reinforcement and independence of ESDP would make third countries take Europe seriously as a world actor; but Europe would not need to emulate the power of the United States. The European Union is not threatened by any organised state and does not have any hegemonic or policing ambitions in the world. In order to become a world player it does not need to have great armed forces, bases and armaments deployed around the globe. It only needs to have **the goodwill of governments and people of the rest of the world** by fostering sustainable development, democracy, multinational integration and the overall respect of international law. These could be the common goals of the unified "common" foreign, commercial, development and defence policies. In an environment of global anarchic terror, this goodwill can be a stronger bulwark against attacks than any global defence system [see section 7.2.10].

7.2.8. Would the political union of Europe entail the loss of national sovereignties for the participating states?

A truly common foreign and security policy, which would be an attribute of the political union of Europe, would certainly entail new transfers of national sovereignties to the Union [see sections

1.2.1 and 3.3.2], but would not mean the loss of the political independence of the participating states. These states **would not necessarily form a federation**. In fact, the very concept of the common policy [see section 1.3.1] excludes the concept of the single policy, which is an attribute of a federation of states. It means that a policy is built up and implemented in common by the common institutions and the governments of the Member States. By implementing a great number of common policies, the Member States of the EC/EU perform certain essential tasks of a state, without forming a single state in the traditional sense. The draft Constitution clearly declares that the Union shall coordinate the policies by which the Member States aim to achieve common objectives, and shall exercise in the Community basis [i.e. method] the competences they confer on it (Art I-1,1). Under the **principle of conferral**, the Union shall act within the limits of the competences conferred upon it by the Member States. Competences not conferred upon the Union in the Constitution remain with the Member States (Art. I-11, 1) [see section 3.3.2].

It ensues from this principle, which has been applied since the beginning of the EC/EU, that each member of the group participating in a real CFSP would keep intact its legal personality and sovereignty in all areas not placed under the common competence of the group. It could sign international agreements not conflicting with Community competence. It could keep its diplomatic representations in third countries and in international institutions. The representations of the members of the group would simply have instructions to follow the positions agreed in common, a fact that would enhance the position of the participating states in world affairs [see section 7.2.7]. In the field of defence as well, each member of the inner group would keep its own army, its armaments and its defence budget. The willing states would only place them under an integrated command, which would be responsible for their coordinated actions. This would not prevent separate actions, compatible with the CFSP, in case of non-agreement by the partners on a common action.

7.2.9. How could some Member States progress towards their political union?

A real CFSP, which is the essential component of political union, could be progressively developed among willing nations with the Community method restrained by the principles of conferral and subsidiarity [see sections 5.2.1, 5.1.1 and 5.1.2]. However, it is practically certain that not all the Member States of the actual EU would be willing to hand over to the Union the competences necessary for building a genuine common foreign and security policy [see section 1.2.1]. Experience to date shows that if the public opinion in some countries is negative on an issue, e.g. the common currency, then, even if they want to, the politicians of those countries cannot follow the common march [see section 6.3.3]. In a Community/Union of twenty-five states, it is quite probable that one government, one parliament or a referendum in one country may stop the march of all the others by vetoing the amendment of a treaty (be it named constitutional or otherwise) [see sections 7.1.7 and 7.2.4].

The question then arises: would the Member States whose citizens aspire to really common foreign and security policies [see section 7.2.6] be forever blocked by their partners who prefer to guard their national prerogatives rather than unite their forces in order to build **a superpower capable of better serving their common interests**? The probable answer is that sooner or later a number of states would, under the pressure of their citizens, want to gain their freedom to proceed to the integration stage of the political union and thus build a truly common foreign and security policy. It is probable that this would be the group of states, which would have a single currency on top of the single market [see sections 6.3.1 and 6.3.4]. The interests of those states would become ever more common and it is natural that sooner rather than later they would feel the need to defend them in common through a genuine common foreign and security policy.

The subsidiary question to the one above is: how would the Member States of the EU, which would want to step up to the stage of political union, be able to do so, as long as the unanimity rule prevails for the amendment of the Treaty on the European Union and as long as some of the signatories of this Treaty do not want to make the conferrals of national sovereignties necessary for taking this step? There are two possible answers to this question. The easier but limited way for building a common foreign and security policy is through the **enhanced cooperation** of some Member States, provided for by the actual Treaty of Nice and reinforced by the Constitutional Treaty [see section 5.2.7]. The more difficult but sturdier way of proceeding to the political union of Europe would be through **a Constitution democratically adopted** in the way suggested above [see section 7.2.4]. If the majority of the members of the constituent assembly, which would draft this Constitution, had a clear mandate from their constituents to provide for a genuinely common foreign and security policy, it should make this provision, giving the freedom to all willing Member States to join in. This freedom would exist, since the Constitution and, hence, the obligations inscribed in it, would concern only the Member States which signed and ratified it.

We would thus have in Europe **a nucleus of States** pursuing their economic, monetary and political integration with the so-called Community method, which should in fact be called the "integration method" in order not to be identified with the Community alone and to be distinguished from the intergovernmental method [see sections 1.2.1 and 5.2.1]. They would be the states which would have signed and ratified the Constitution or an enhanced co-operation agreement on the CFSP and would, thus, have marked their willingness to integrate their economic, monetary, security and foreign policies and thus create among themselves over and above the common market, an economic and monetary union and a political union. The States in the **second concentric circle** would remain at the stage of the common market as long as they wished and would be welcome to join the inner circle when they were willing and ready to do so by ratifying the Constitution or an enhanced cooperation agreement concerning the CFSP.

Of course, this situation would not be ideal since it would entail institutional problems. However, **institutional solutions already exist concerning monetary affairs** [see sections 6.3.3 and 6.3.6]. They could be extended to foreign affairs. New legislation obtained with the abstention of Member States which had not ratified the Constitution should not be binding on them until ratification, but should be implemented by them thereafter. Intergovernmental co-operation, in particular through the open coordination method, employing non-binding measures such as resolutions and recommendations could be used in a complementary way by both groups of states, according to the principles of subsidiarity and proportionality [see sections 1.2.2, 5.1.2 and 5.1.3].

7.2.10. What would be the relations of politically united European states with third countries?

In addition to the two circles of states pursuing their integration up to different points - all up to the point of the common market and some up to the point of the foreign and security policy - we would have the outer circle of **the European Economic Area** practising free trade through intergovernmental cooperation [see section 2.2.3]. This circle - now limited to the EC/EU states, Norway, Iceland and Liechtenstein - could one day be widened to include Russia and other States of the former Soviet block having espoused an open market economy and wishing to have strong links with the European Community/Union. All these countries should, of course, belong to the large **European family** having the same values, similar democratic institutions and common ideals. With non-European countries in its periphery - i.e. Mediterranean countries in Asia and Africa, which have different cultures, traditions and regimes - the European Community/Union should build strong economic and political links through **partnership and/or new neighbourhood agreements**. A task of the common foreign and security policy of the Union would be to coordinate the commercial, aid to development and foreign policies of the Member States of the Union so as to create a friendly and therefore secure area around Europe, notably in the Mediterranean and the Middle East.

The links which the European Union would have with the European countries in the outer circle and with friendly countries in other regions of the world would make it **a world player of prime importance**, basing the prestige and security of its members less on the force of arms and more on their assistance for the durable development of friendly countries [see section 7.2.7]. In a world which aspires to peace, social justice, economic progress and the rule of law, it is extremely important that a democratic and pluralistic Europe, with no expansionist ambitions, assumes the international role endowed upon it by its history, its culture and economic power. Its successful experiment of a peaceful and voluntary integration of nations, which only yesterday were fighting each other [see section 1.1], is being watched closely by many nations throughout the world suffering from their ethnic, religious and other conflicts and could place the old continent at **the vanguard of the march of civilisation**, whose main objectives are world peace, political freedom, economic progress and social justice.

Indeed, if "Civilisation" is taken to mean an advanced system of human values and social development guaranteeing peace, freedom of opinion and welfare for all persons, civilisation is not yet enjoyed by a huge part of mankind. In this sense of civilisation, multinational integration may be considered the **most important socio-political invention since the invention of democracy**, because it spreads and consolidates the values of the latter: the rule of law, the separation of the state from religion, freedom of initiative, equality of nations and individuals, well distributed welfare for all regions and social categories. These capital socio-political discoveries, which go hand in hand (since the concept of integration is inseparable from that of democracy) [see section 1.1.1], were made on

European soil. It is true that Europe also invented colonialism, racism, fascism, bolshevism and other "isms", but these bad inventions ended in failures and are currently disavowed by the immense majority of Europeans. On the other hand, Europeans have a vital reason to promote the models of democracy, humanism and integration that they have developed and are still improving, to the nations that are torn apart and starving, exploited by crooked demagogues and plutocrats of all kinds bearing all sorts of fancy banners. The reason is the **protection of their own safety and wellbeing** from all these false prophets.